MW01101194

Flours and Grains for Feasting is published by
WHITEHEART WORKERS CO-OP LTD.
38 Humber Crescent, Tauranga
New Zealand

Copyright © Whiteheart Workers Co-op 1989

First Edition 1989

This book was designed and lasertypeset by
*Artful Design,*Tauranga
New Zealand.

Illustrations and cover: *Adi Tait*
Text: *Tim Mulcock*

ISBN 0-473-00739-8

Printed by Monographics Ltd.,
Auckland, New Zealand

DEDICATION

Flours and Grains for Feasting
is dedicated to the True Heart of Love
Who is the Brightest Spirit Force of Compassionate Understanding
(who is God, who You are).

MANY THANKS

Very many people have helped with the adventure of
Whiteheart Co-op, the flour mills, the bakery and this recipe book.
Lots of time and advice has been given freely by all kinds of people.
We are very grateful. Thank you all.

THE WHITEHEART TIGER

(or the true nature of sacrifice)

A long time ago in a jungle in India lived a wandering monk. He spent his days in simple rituals of prayer and food gathering.

One day as he was collecting fresh herbs he came to a clearing and noticed a huge tiger lying in the shade on the far side. The tiger barely moved at his appearance and the monk realised that the tiger was too weak to move.

Struck by compassion for the magnificent creature the monk moved slowly to its side. Realising the tiger was weak from hunger he made a cut in his hand and tried to drip the blood into its mouth. The sustenance was too little and the tiger was too weak to swallow. It seemed the tiger would die.

Briefly considering things and moved by a steady impulse from his heart, the monk quickly slit his own throat and, pulling open the tiger's jaws, lay down with his throat in the animal's mouth.

CONTENTS

INTRODUCTION

    Wild seed-bearing grasses were one of early man's main food sources. Grain has been a part of our diet for over 40,000 years.

    Foraging for wild grain determined pre-historic man an isolated, mobile existence. With the domestication of these wild crops some 10,000 years ago primeval man was able to remain in one area and harvest bigger crops. From these beginnings the first village communities were established.

    Co-operation and teamwork were essential skills developed by these people to prepare the land, plant the seed, tend the growing plants and to harvest the grain.

    In many parts of the world today physical survival is no longer under direct threat and the skills of co-operation and teamwork have been neglected.

    There is an urgency for these skills to be rediscovered, perhaps not for our physical survival, but for the survival of our true nature as intelligent, compassionate beings whose fulfilment is in relationship.

WHITEHEART CO-OP

Several years ago in a town called Wellington in the land of New Zealand, a cook, a computer programmer, a gardener and a musician got together to form a company to do good things.

Our idea was to make an experimental model of a cooperative business in which we shared responsibility, work and rewards.

From our interest in the local Organic Food Co-op (a cooperative supermarket specialising in organically grown food) we saw a need for organically grown flours and processed food.

We pooled our money, borrowed from friends and bought a small stonegrinding flour mill.

To start with we milled fresh wholemeal and specialty flours for the Organic Food Co-op and the local healthfood shops and supermarkets. For a while we experimented with organic relishes, chutneys, pickles and marmalades but the quantity we could produce was too small to be viable so we decided to concentrate on stonemilling fresh flours and baking bread, vegetarian pies and biscuits with the flours.

Several of the original partners left, new people became involved; as partners, employees, volunteer workers, or by offering other assistance or finance.

We reached a point where we could no longer do our own

5

marketing, distribution and delivery as well as keeping up with the milling, packing and baking.

After talks with friends in a health food distribution business in Tauranga, several hundred miles north, we decided to move Whiteheart to Tauranga, next door to Harmony Natural Foods who would distribute our products nationally.

Everything was loaded into two big freight containers and railed to Tauranga. We followed in our old rusty Hiace van, packed to the roof with clothes and saucepans.

Once we set up expansion was rapid. Within several months we had increased our sales and stock by ten times, and opened our own bakery and wholefoods shop.

Although the business grew successfully the co-operative ideal struggled. It was hard to find new partners; newcomers preferred to be employees. We wrestled with the constitution trying to allow it to reflect the various degrees of commitment people could afford to put in.

Eventually it seemed we were no longer operating as a co-operative and had assumed the conventional model of a small business; privately owned with employed staff.

After months of unsuccessfully advertising for partners and faced with continued expansion and the unwelcome employer/ employee relationship, we decided to sell the business.

Luckily Harmony Natural Foods stepped in and bought the flour mill and bakery and is continuing our work making fresh organic flours available through a new company, Chico Mills Ltd.

We had been developing a graphic design studio as a separate division of Whiteheart with the skills of one of the later partners, Adi Tait. After the flour mills and bakery were sold we expanded it into a full time business, calling it Artful Design.

With our new resources we were at last able to collate the mountain of recipes we had collected. This recipe book is the result. We hope you find it useful and enjoy the food.

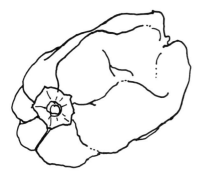 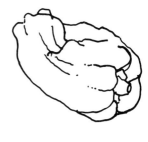

ORGANICALLY GROWN

Although many people testify to the toxic effects of chemical fertilisers, herbicides and pesticides on their health, and feel completely relieved on a diet of organically grown food, our interest in organically grown food has its base in the wider context of land management and environmental balance.

What is organically grown?

Organic and biological husbandry are terms describing land management techniques that co-exist with the processes of the wider environment. No chemical pesticides, fertilisers or herbicides are used. Crop quality is maintained by harmonising with natural cycles and systems. Varieties are selected that can grow successfully outside the artificial shelter of spray programmes and chemical land management techniques.

Synthetic horticultural chemicals are an expensive and ecologically unsuitable short-cut for growing food.

Artificial fertilisers bypass important links, for the plants, with the humus of the soil. The effect of this is damaged soil structure which leads to excess nutrients washing off the land and polluting our lakes, rivers and oceans. The damaged soil structure also leads to soil compaction and the collapse of soil texture. The soil turns to dust and blows away in the wind.

Chemical pesticides and herbicides kill beneficial plants, insects, fungi and bacteria, along with the unwanted ones. The poisoning of any step in the food chain has a profound effect on the whole system.

The fundamental practise of organic husbandry is the addition of composted animal and vegetable wastes to enrich the soil. This keeps the soil structure stable and the plant growth healthy and strong. There are several different methods of organic land management. Two of the most widely supported are Permaculture and Biodynamics.

An international group, I.F.O.A.M. (the International Federation of Organic Agriculture Movements) supports research and provides international standards which rule on the types of substances and methods that may be used.

Many countries and groups of growers have organised standards from this basis and allow growers who conform to the standards to use a certified organic trademark. The Biodynamic Association has the international "Demeter" trademark which it allows approved members to use.

FLOUR MILLING

Fresh milled flours are best. Not only is it much better food but it also tastes better. If you have the time to mill your own grain, several small flour mills are available for home use. Otherwise buy fresh milled (preferably organically grown) flours from your local healthfood shop or supermarket. Some of the flours and grains can be hard to obtain at various times. We suggest asking frequently at your local healthfood shop or writing to a healthfood wholesaler in your area.

Wholegrain flours are a more complete food as the nutritional and digestive qualities of the oils, bran and vitamins are retained in the flour. Although a significant proportion of these nutritional qualities are lost with conventional stonegrinding mills almost all are lost with conventional roller milling.

Extra-fine Wholemeal Flour now available

A stonemilling process recently developed in Germany allows the production of even better flours. A fan blows the grain against a granite milling stone, gradually wearing the whole grain to powder. The process is so gentle that milling temperatures remain low and a high proportion of oils and vitamins are retained. The keeping qualities of the flours are enhanced by this process as the

constant air current ensures flours have very low moisture content.
    Although at present it is a slow process, the flour produced is as fine as so-called *white* flour. This extra-fine wholemeal flour is 100% wholegrain and can be used to bake light sponges, croissants and pastries. We recommend it. At last the image of solid, crumbly wholemeal-brick-bread and slab scones can be laid to rest.

SPROUTING GRAINS AND SEEDS

Sprouted grains and seeds have been part of man's diet for thousands of years. Although they are still part of the traditional diet of many Eastern cultures, sprouts have gained a huge increase in popularity in the West in the last thirty years.
    Sprouts are nutritional miracles. As germination occurs a flow of energy is triggered that produces enzymes which change the carbohydrates into digestible sugars; complex proteins are converted into simpler amino acids; and fats become more digestible fatty acids. Vitamins are produced and minerals and other trace elements are absorbed and combined with the amino acids making them available to our bodies.
    As a raw food, sprouts are unexcelled for vitality and flavour. Even as a cooked food they add delicious flavour and texture and can be used when other fresh vegetables are expensive or out of season.

How to Sprout Grains

Here are some general guides to sprouting your own. Some grains prefer slightly different conditions; these details are included under *Uses and Preparation*, for each grain.

Soak the grain in water for about 8 hours. Drain and put them into a jar covered with a piece of muslin.

Rinse the sprouts twice a day (more often in hot weather). Sprouted grains are at their best when the shoot is about the same length as the grain itself. This usually takes 2 to 4 days.

SOAK GRAIN

DRAIN AND COVER WITH MUSLIN

RINSE SPROUTS TWICE A DAY

SHOOT SHOULD BE THE SAME LENGTH AS THE GRAIN

GLUTEN FREE THICKENERS AND BINDERS

Buckwheat flour, pea flour and linseed are good replacements for wheat flour and eggs in breads, biscuits and pancakes. Pea flour, because of its characteristic flavour, is more suited to savoury foods.

Mashed banana and mashed avocado are also good binders for breads, muffins, patties, pancakes, biscuits and cakes.

Millet flour, pea flour, sago and tapioca are all good wheat-free thickeners, especially good in soups, stews and casseroles.

Linseed for thickening and binding

1/2 cup whole linseed
1 1/2 cups of water

Bring the linseed and the water to the boil. Simmer for 5-10 minutes stirring constantly until the mixture thickens. Add this to your recipes in place of eggs or wheat flour. The flavour is neutral and it is simple to make.

ALTERNATIVE BAKING POWDER
Wheat and Sodium Free

The discovery of yeast was a breakthrough for the Egyptians but today we often look for alternatives to yeasted leavening. Maybe the flavour is too strong, or we have a yeast intolerance or perhaps we are in a hurry.

Baking Powder is not an ideal solution, the bicarbonate of soda destroys the B vitamins while producing the carbon-dioxide that raises the dough and the sodium that usually forms part of the bicarbonate is toxic to our bodies. The following recipe is far from perfect but you can be sure you are getting no wheat based filler or sodium. All leavenings should be used with moderation.

1 cup of arrowroot powder
1 cup of cream of tartar
1/2 cup of potassium bicarbonate

Mix ingredients together and store in an airtight container. Remix before using.Most pharmacies have potassium bicarbonate.

11

OILS FOR COOKING AND SALADS

Extracted oils always involve some compromise. The best way to ingest oils is to eat the seed or bean from which the oil is extracted. This way the oils are fresh and balanced for the body's system.

However extracted oils are now a deeply rooted part of our culinary heritage. We recommend always using unrefined oils, not only because they have more goodness in them but also because they have more flavour.

In raw food dishes unrefined cold-pressed oils are a cut above other oils and light and fresh on the palate. But for cooking, cold-pressed oils are unnecessary as the higher quality is lost when the oil is heated.

Each of the oils has a distinctive character and flavour. Safflower and sunflower oils are popular for their mild flavour which gives them versatility for sweet and savoury dishes. Olive oil is traditionally used for salads and the cooking of savoury dishes. Corn oil is a beautiful golden colour with a rich mellow flavour, it is high in vitamin E and natural anti-oxidants. Peanut oil has a distinctive flavour which is suitable for some savoury dishes but probably not sweets. Sesame oil is generally expensive but it has a delicious flavour suitable for a range of raw, cooked, savoury and sweet dishes. It also has the advantage of an ingredient called *sesamol* which keeps the oil stable and free from rancidity.

WHEAT

Description

Wheat is a member of the *Triticum* family of grasses, it was one of the earliest to be domesticated. It is easily hybridised and hundreds of cultivars are now available so that wheat can be grown in a wide range of different climates and conditions. The colour of the grain ranges from a dark red-brown (purple wheat) to pale yellow or blonde grains. The size and shape of the grain varies between varieties too.

Wheat is the most widely consumed crop throughout the world. Its popularity as a food source stems from the unique capacity the protein has to form an elastic gluten when mixed with water. Yeast and sugar added to this release carbon dioxide which is trapped by the elastic gluten. The effect of this is to lift the dough, producing light, airy baked products.

Several other advantages have ensured wheat an enduring place in our diet. The grain yields highly compared with other cereal grains. Disease resistant cultivars have been bred lowering the risk of crop failure. Wheat stores very well for years (even for thousands of years; wheat stored in tombs in the Eygptian pyramids was sprouted some 5,000 years later). Wheat is also a good source of nutrition and usable protein compared with other grains.

The varieties are grouped into hard and soft wheats. This description arises from the structure of the grains and the way they fracture in the milling process. A hard wheat fractures through the protein cell walls. These wheats have properties giving elastic doughs suitable for yeasted breads. Soft wheats, however, fracture along the lines of the cell walls. These wheats are generally lower in protein and are more suitable for biscuits, cakes and unyeasted pastries.

The best hard wheats of the world are grown in hot, dry conditions. Most of the world's hard wheat is grown in Australia, Russia, America and parts of Canada. *Durum* wheat is a particularly hard variety used exclusively for making pasta.

Soft wheats are grown in more moderate climates and are often blended with harder wheats for a more versatile flour.

History

Wheat has been a food source of man for over 10,000 years. The earliest evidence dates back to about 8000 BC in the area of the Tigris-Euphrates valleys, in the eastern Mediterranean. By 4000 BC the Eygptians had discovered the use of yeast as a leavening for wheat breads and were baking fancy high-rise coiled and plaited loaves. By 2500 BC a flourishing wheat industry was established in the Middle East. Farmers from the Tigris-Euphrates valleys exported wheat throughout the known world. The Roman Empire spread the cultivation of wheat as it expanded. Wheat formed a staple part of the diet of the Roman Army.

It was not until the late Middle Ages, several hundred centuries later, that the popularity of wheat spread rapidly. The more technologically inclined societies began to favour highly processed white wheat flour as a status symbol while traditional peasant foods and recipes were scorned. It is only within the last 30 years nutrition, flavour and texture have regained popular approval as the criteria for good bread.

Unleavened breads and flatbreads were the earliest recipes for wheat flour. These breads are still a major part of the diet in the Middle East and India.

Uses and Preparation

Although the flour is the best known food from the wheat plant, the benefits of the juice from wheatgrass and the taste and texture of the sprouted grain are a superb addition to any diet.

Wheat is comparatively low in the amino acid, *lysine*. For a balanced protein include 30% pulses with your wheat dishes.

Wheat flours are suitable for a wide range of breads, biscuits, cakes, sauces and pastries.

With the introduction of the new extra-fine wholemeal flours (see *Flour Milling* on page 8), sponges, pastries and light breads can now be made with a flour that is 100% wholegrain and also milled at room temperature.

14

RAW GRAIN MUESLI (Raw)
Chewy, nourishing tiger-food.

1/2 cup of whole wheat
1/2 cup of fresh oatmeal
1 cup of water
1 cup of yogurt
2 oranges, peeled and chopped
1 cup of grapes
1 chopped banana

Soak the wheat and the oatmeal overnight.
Drain and mix the grain in a bowl with the other ingredients.
Serve with a slice of lemon and perhaps honey.

Serves 2-4.

REJUVELAC (Raw)
This is a revitalising drink with a lemony tang .

1/2 cup of soft pastry wheat
5 cups of water

Soak the wheat for about 12 hours. Drain and let the wheat sprout for 1 day. Mince the wheat sprouts and pour into a 2-litre flask with the 5 cups of water. Cover firmly with a piece of muslin.
Let this stand for 3 days. Drain off the liquid - this is the rejuvelac, and serve as an invigorating tonic on its own or as a base for salad dressings.

WINTER WHEAT PORRIDGE

1/2 cup of flaked or kibbled wheat
2 cups of cold water
1 cup of chopped fresh fruit
1/2 cup of raisins
1 tsp of honey
1/2 cup of fresh goat's milk or soymilk
1/2 tsp of mixed spice

Stir the wheat cereal into the water and slowly bring to the boil, stirring frequently. Cover and simmer on a low heat for 20 minutes, stirring occasionally. Add the fruit, raisins, honey and spice. Mix in well and serve with milk.

 Serves 2.

TOMATOES STUFFED WITH WHEAT SPROUTS (Raw)

6 large tomatoes
2 cups of sprouted wheat
1/2 cup of chopped parsley
1/4 cup of chopped celery
1/4 cup of chopped fresh basil
1/2 cup of blue vein cheese
1/4 cup of mayonnaise

Slice the tops off the tomatoes and place to one side. Scoop out the insides of the tomatoes with a spoon (use this pulp in a cold soup perhaps).

Mix the remaining ingredients together in a bowl and fill each tomato with the mixture. Replace the tomato tops and serve.

Serves 6.

SPROUTED WHEAT AND RED PEPPER SALAD (Raw)
A colourful exotic-looking salad.

1 cup of sprouted wheat
1 chopped red pepper
1 cup of sliced fresh mushrooms
1/3 cup of chopped fresh basil
1/3 cup of chopped fresh mint
1/3 cup of chopped fresh parsley
1 tbsp of unsalted food yeast
juice of 1/2 lemon
1/2 cup of yogurt or soft tofu
paprika

Toss all the ingredients except the paprika together in a large bowl. Sprinkle the paprika over the top as a garnish and serve.
Remember the sprouts are best when the growing tip is no longer than the length of the grain.
This salad is delicious with sprouted rye, triticale or oats in place of sprouted wheat.

Serves 2-4.

WHEAT SPROUT PATTIES

These patties have a fragrance reminiscent of Arabian Nights with a sweet nutty flavour and delicious texture.

2 cups of sprouted wheat
1/2 cup of buckwheat flour
1 tsp of ground cumin
2 tsps of turmeric
1 tsp of ground coriander
1/4 tsp of cayenne
1 tsp of cinnamon
2 tbsps of unrefined sesame oil
cooking oil
about 1/2 cup of water

Mince or finely chop the sprouted wheat. Sauté the remaining ingredients with the sesame oil in a pan for about 2 minutes. Mix together with the minced wheat sprouts and the water and beat into a stiff batter.

Drop dessertspoonfuls of batter into a pan with a small amount of cooking oil at a medium heat. Smooth the patties to about 1cm thick with a spoon and fry for several minutes on each side. Serve with a mixed salad.

Makes 10 patties.

TABOULI

Bulgur wheat is a traditional Middle Eastern preparation of wheat. The wheat is kibbled, cooked then dried.

1 1/2 cups of bulgur wheat
1 cup of chopped spring onions
3 chopped tomatoes
1 chopped cucumber
1 1/2 cups of chopped parsley
1/2 cup of lemon juice
1/4 cup of olive oil
4 cups of boiling water

Pour the boiling water over the bulgur wheat and leave for 1 hour. Drain the excess water, mix in the other ingredients and chill before serving.

Serve on a bed of shredded lettuce or spinach.

Serves 6.

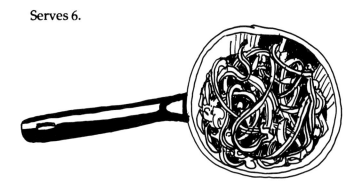

REAL NOODLES
Absolutely delectable - the difference between these noodles and commercial dried noodles is so great a row of planets would barely stretch half-way.

4 cups of Durum wheat flour (or hard wheat flour)
about 1/2 cup of water
1/2 tsp of salt (optional)

Gradually add the water to the flour (and the salt) in a bowl, mixing into a dry dough. Knead for 15 minutes, then roll out on to a floured board to a sheet about 1mm thick or less. Fold the edges of the sheet into the middle and then fold once more to give four layers.

Cut the folded sheet into strips about 2mm wide with a sharp knife. Bring a large saucepan of water to the boil and unroll each noodle before lowering it into the water. Bring to the boil again and simmer until the noodles are cooked - about 10 minutes.

Drain and rinse in cold running water. Serve with tomato and basil or a cheese sauce.

Serves 4-6 people.

SPROUTS SUPREME (Raw)

1 cup of sprouted wheat
1 cup of chopped pecans, walnuts,
   sunflower seeds or a mixture
1 cup of raisins
1 tbsp of honey
fine shredded coconut

Chop or mince the sprouts and raisins, then mix with the chopped nuts and seeds and honey.
Form into 4cm balls by hand and roll in the coconut. Chill before serving.

Makes 10-12 balls.

RAW FRUIT CAKE (Raw)
A heavenly cake. Mince the fruit finely to get thin slices.

1 cup of sprouted wheat
1/2 cup of raisins
1/2 cup of dates
1/2 cup of dried apricots
1/2 cup of dried apple
1/2 cup of dried figs
1/2 cup of dried banana
1/2 cup of sliced almonds
1/2 cup of coconut cream

Mince the sprouted wheat, dried fruit and nuts. Press firmly into a bread tin. Pour the coconut cream over the top. Chill for 24 hours and serve thinly sliced.

Makes 1 loaf.

CROISSANTS

4 cups of extra-fine hard wholemeal flour
250 g of cold butter
1/2 tsp of salt (optional)
1 1/2 cups of warm water, milk or soymilk
2 tsps active dried yeast

Stir the yeast into the warm water and leave to stand for 20 minutes until frothy. Mix the flour (and salt) with the yeast liquid and knead for about 10 minutes into a soft dough. Place in a bowl, cover and leave to rise for 1 hour. Punch down the dough, sprinkle it with flour, wrap it in a plastic bag and refrigerate for 1 hour.

Roll the dough into an oblong. Slice half the butter thinly and spread over two-thirds of the dough. Fold the unbuttered third to the middle and then fold again, making three layers. Roll this out into an oblong again, slice the remaining butter and lay on the dough in the same way. Fold the dough as before, wrap in plastic again and refrigerate for 1-2 hours to keep the butter from melting through the layers.

Roll the pastry out 3mm thick to a width of 15cm and cut diagonally every 15cm. Roll up each triangle from the short side (see diagram). Bend the roll into a crescent shape and place on a baking tray with the point underneath. Chill for 1 hour.

Bake for 10 minutes at 245° C (475° F) then lower the temperature to 190°C (375°F) and bake for a further 10-15 minutes.

Makes about 1 dozen croissants.

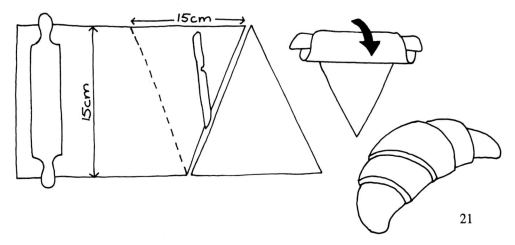

ESSENE BREAD

This is a traditional bread from Israel. In the hot dry climate of that region the recipe consisted solely of ground sprouts mixed with water. This dough was then sunbaked in the open air.
Our version has buckwheat flour to help bind it and make it slice more easily. The addition of buckwheat also means the bread has a complete protein balance in itself. We also recommend oven baking. This is a simple, sweet, delicious bread.

> 3 cups of sprouted wheat
> 1 cup of buckwheat flour
> water

Mince, grind or chop the sprouts finely and mix with the buckwheat flour. Knead for 5-10 minutes into a sticky dough, adding water only if necessary. Either form into round loaves or press into an oiled bread tin. Bake at 175°C (350°F) for 1 1/2 hours.

Makes 1 loaf.

LEBANESE PITTA BREAD

These flatbreads puff up to make a pocket, ideal for salad sandwiches with the raw chutney recipe following.

> 5-6 cups of wholemeal flour
> 1 tbsp of active dried yeast
> 2 cups of warm water
> 1 tsp of honey
> pinch of salt (optional)
> 1/2 cup sesame seeds (optional)

Mix the yeast and honey into the warm water and leave for 15 minutes.

Add the flour (and salt) and knead well into a soft dough. Cover and leave to rise for 1 hour. Punch down and divide into 12 balls. Roll each ball out on a floured board into a round about 3mm thick. Place on lightly floured baking trays and leave in a warm place to rise for 45 minutes. Turn the bread after 20 minutes.

Bake at 230°C (450°F) for 5-8 minutes, until lightly browned.

Makes 12.

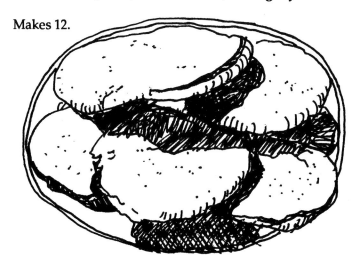

RAW FRUIT CHUTNEY (Raw)

1/4 cup of chopped dates
1/4 cup of chopped raisins
1/2 cup of chopped onion
3 chopped tomatoes
1 chopped apple
1 tsp grated fresh ginger
1/2 tsp of allspice
1/4 tsp of mace
1/2 tsp of cracked mustard seeds
1/2 cup of cider vinegar

Mix the ingredients thoroughly.
Serve with salad as a filling for pitta bread or sandwiches.
This chutney keeps for about a week if refrigerated.

ARABIAN SPINACH PIES

pitta bread dough (see recipe on page 22)
500 g of fresh spinach
2 finely chopped onions
1/4 cup of unrefined olive oil
1/2 tsp of allspice
1/4 cup of raisins
juice of 2 lemons

Make the pitta bread dough as in the recipe but using TWICE the amount of yeast. Leave the dough to rise for 1-2 hours until doubled in bulk.

Cook the spinach very lightly and drain off as much liquid as possible. Sauté the onion in the olive oil and add to the spinach with the other ingredients. Cook over a low heat for 5-10 minutes. Leave to cool.

Form 12 balls and roll out to 10cm rounds, about 3mm thick. Spoon a tablespoon of filling on to the centre of each.

Lift the edge of each round from three places and press together to form a three-sided pyramid.

Pre-heat the oven to 205° C (400° F) and bake the pies for about 15 minutes until lightly browned.

Mashed chickpeas with lemon juice and parsley are also delectable as a filling.

Makes about 12 pies.

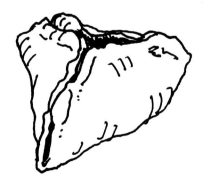

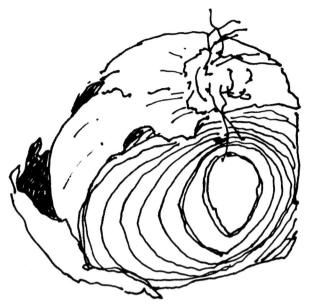

SYRIAN HERBY CRISPBREAD

4 cups of wholemeal flour
2 tsps of baking powder (see alternative on page 11)
1 finely chopped onion
1 tsp of dried thyme
1/2 tsp of cumin powder
1/2 tsp of ground coriander
1/4 tsp of cayenne
1/3 cup of olive oil
1 1/2 cups of water

Mix the flour (and baking powder) in a bowl. Add the remaining ingredients, except the water, and combine well.

Add the water slowly to form a smooth pliable dough. Knead the dough on a floured board for 15-20 minutes. Divide the dough into eight and roll each into a round 2-3mm thick.

Dust with flour, cover and leave to rise for 10 minutes. Preheat the oven to 260° C (500° F). Put the breads on to lightly oiled baking trays and cook for 5-10 minutes until the tops start to brown. Remove from the oven and allow to cool before serving.

Makes 8 rounds.

CHAPATI

These pan-fried flatbreads are the basis of the daily Indian vegetarian meal. They are a good, simple, non-greasy, non-yeasty bread.

4 cups of wholemeal flour
water

Mix flour with enough water to make an elastic dough and knead for a few minutes. Let stand for 10 minutes, then knead again. More water may have to be added to keep the dough soft and workable.

Divide the dough into 12 pieces. Roll each into a ball, flatten and roll on a floured surface into 15cm diameter rounds.

Heat a solid-bottomed pan until very hot. Cook each flatbread without oil, turning after about 10 seconds. Cook the second side for about 20 seconds until brown spots appear.

The chapati will puff up if you press it lightly back into the pan. It is traditionally served with a coating of ghee (clarified butter) and a vegetarian curry or dhal.

Makes 12.

RICE

Description

Rice is a grass having a seed very similar in structure to the wheat grain. Most rice grows in semi-aquatic conditions in paddy fields, although there are varieties that grow on dry land. A high proportion of the nutrients in rice are contained in the outer layers which are removed for polished or white rice. Containing no gluten, rice is one of the least allergenic of the grains.

Varieties of rice vary enormously. Some mature at two feet tall, others grow to five feet. The different varieties suit a range of climatic and culinary conditions. Rice is broadly divided into two categories: short-grained varieties, which have higher yields and tend to be regarded as dessert rices, and long-grained varieties, which are usually preferred by rice eating cultures. Long-grain rice tends to remain as separate grains after cooking whereas short-grain rice often becomes soft, gelatinous and sticky after cooking.

A third group, wild rice, is a loose description for several different grains, from a purple rice variant which has a startling colour but no special flavour attraction to the connoisseurs' wild rice which has long slender grains and an unusual nutty flavour. This grain is not strictly a rice at all. It is a semi-aquatic grass and is still largely harvested by hand in the wild from the shores of various lakes. Nutritionally it is superior to rice with a high well-balanced protein content.

History

Rice was itself a wild crop harvested in this same way for thousands of years before it was domesticated. It was harvested from the wild in its native areas of India and South-East Asia from about 6000 BC but it was not until about 3000 BC in India that it was sown as a domestic crop. From this time however rice growing spread rapidly east into China and the Yangtse Valley where it was a well established crop by 2000 BC. From these areas rice growing spread throughout Persia and the Middle East and by 1000 BC it was a popular food of the Greeks. The Moors introduced rice to

Spain during the medieval wars and from here it spread into France and Italy.

Rice was first grown in America around 1700 AD. Commercial rice growing increased rapidly and today America is one of the main rice exporting countries.

Uses and Preparation

Brown rice is one of the most easily digested grains. It is also digested more slowly than other grains making it more sustaining.

Brown rice sprouts are delicious and versatile. They can be used as an alternative to wheat sprouts in any dish. Only whole grain brown rice that has not been heat-treated will sprout successfully.

The use of the cooked whole grain is well known, however the value and versatility of brown rice flour deserves to be more widely recognised. The flour is mild and fine suiting both sweet and savoury dishes. It makes good gravies and sauces.

Brown rice flour piecrusts and biscuits are excellent. However breads with large proportions of rice flour will tend to crumble. Dryness with cakes and breads using rice flour can be alleviated by replacing 1/4 of the flour with ground nuts, fresh or soaked dried fruit or grated carrots.

RICE SPROUT BREAKFAST (Raw)

1 cup of rice sprouts
1 cup of fresh chopped pineapple
1/2 cup of muscatel raisins
150g of soft tofu
grated coconut

Mince the rice sprouts and the raisins and mix with the other ingredients. Serve with a topping of grated coconut.

Serves 2.

RICE TEMPURA

A simple treat with a rare exquisite subtlety. Served elegantly with a wedge of lemon and garnished with parsley, rice tempura equals the finest dishes of the world.

2 cups of wholemeal flour
2 cups of cooked brown rice
about 1 cup of water
cooking oil
wedges of lemon
fresh parsley
unsalted food yeast and kelp (optional)

Mix the flour and rice into a thick batter with the water. Fry the batter by the tablespoonful in hot oil for about 3 minutes, until golden brown.

Remove the tempura with tongs and drain well. Keep in a warm oven until it is all cooked.

Serve with wedges of lemon and a parsley garnish. This dish is enhanced with a sprinkling of unsalted food yeast and kelp powder.

Makes about 20 pieces.

ALMOND FRIED RICE
A superb gourmet rice dish full of nutty crunch and protein.

2 cups of slightly undercooked brown rice
1/2 cup of chopped pistachio nuts
1/2 cup of chopped almonds
1/2 cup of chopped cashews
1/2 tsp of ground nutmeg
1/4 cup of cooking oil
1/2 cup of chopped fresh parsley
1 cup of water

Sauté the nuts in the oil for 2 minutes then stir in the rice and nutmeg. Add the water and simmer for 10 minutes. Remove from the heat, mix in the chopped parsley and serve.

Makes enough for 4.

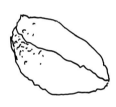

FRESH HERBED RICE
Simple, easy and great tasting.

2 cups of rice
1/2 cup of chopped parsley
1 tbsp fresh chopped basil
1 tbsp fresh chopped chives
1 minced clove of garlic

Boil the rice with 5 cups of water for about 30 minutes until cooked. Remove from the heat and drain.
Lightly mix in the herbs and garlic then serve.

Makes plenty for 4.

DANISH RICE PUDDING

3 cups of cooked short-grain dessert rice
1 cup of soaked muscatel raisins
2 cups of fresh chopped strawberries (or grapes)
1/2 tsp of ground nutmeg
1/4 tsp of ground cloves
3/4 tsp of ground allspice
300g of soft tofu
(or 1 cup of full cream, or plain yogurt)
chopped nuts

Mix everything together, except the fresh fruit and nuts, including the liquid from the muscatels. Lightly stir in the fresh fruit and mashed tofu, chill and serve with a garnish of chopped nuts.

Although this is a delicious filling summer feast, it can also be served as a hot dish to see you through a cold Danish winter. In this case boil 1 cup of uncooked rice for about 20 minutes, add the raisins and spice and continue to cook for another 10 minutes, until the rice is cooked.

Mash the tofu and blend it into the mixture. Remove from the heat, lightly mix in the fruit and serve hot with soymilk, milk, yogurt or fruit juice and a garnish of chopped nuts.

Makes enough for 4.

CINNAMON RICE PUDDING
Creamy and spicy.

1 1/2 cups of cooked dessert rice
1/4 cup of brown rice flour
1/2 cup of honey or rice malt
2 cups of soy or cow's milk
1 tsp of ground cinnamon
1/2 tsp of pure vanilla essence

Stir all the ingredients together. Place in a covered casserole and bake at 160° C (325° F) for 45 minutes.

Serves 4.

SAVOURY RICE BISCUITS
A chewy snack.

2 1/2 cups of cooked brown rice
1 1/2 cups of brown rice flour
1/2 cup of arrowroot or soy flour
1/2 cup of tahini
1 tbsp finely chopped garlic
1 tbsp of dried mixed herbs
1/2 cup sesame seeds
1/2 cup of water

Mix the ingredients thoroughly together. Press 1/2cm deep into a biscuit tray dusted with rice flour and sesame seeds. Bake at 175° C (350° F) for 50 minutes, until lightly browned.

Cut into squares while hot but leave them to cool completely before removing them from the tray.

Makes about 20.

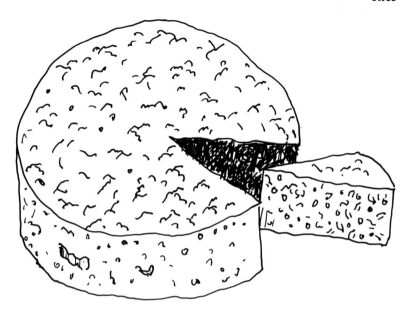

UNLEAVENED RICE FLOUR CARROT CAKE
Rich , moist and healthy - with a lovely texture and appearance.

1 1/2 cups of brown rice flour
2 tsps cinnamon
1 cup of finely chopped sunflower seeds
1/4 cup of arrowroot powder
2 cups of grated carrot
1/2 cup of chopped cashew nuts and/or sliced almonds
1/4 tsp natural vanilla essence
1 cup of fruit juice

Mix the flour, cinnamon, sunflower seeds and arrowroot together. Stir in the carrot, nuts and vanilla essence. Add the fruit juice and mix well into a thick batter.

Tip the batter into a well-oiled breadtin and bake at 180°C (350°F) for 90-100 minutes.

Remove from the oven, cool in the tin for 20 minutes before de-tinning. Wait until it is cold before slicing otherwise it tends to crumble.

RICE FLOUR BANANA MUFFINS
Sweet little cakes.

1 cup of brown rice flour
2 tsp of baking powder (see alternative on page 11)
1 mashed banana
1 tbsp unrefined sunflower oil
2/3 cup of soymilk (or milk)

Mix the dry ingredients together, then add the mashed banana, oil and soymilk. Stir together until lightly mixed. Spoon the batter into an oiled muffin tray and bake at 230° C (450° F) for 12-15 minutes.

Makes 12 muffins.

SAVOURY SESAME RICE CRACKERS

2 cups of brown rice flour
1/2 cup of sesame seeds
1 cup of tahini
150g of soft tofu
3-5 cloves of garlic finely chopped or minced
1/2 cup of water
grated cheese (optional)

Mix everything but the cheese thoroughly. Press the mixture out onto a baking tray, well dusted with rice flour, to a thickness of about 5mm. Cut into cracker-size strips with a wet knife. Grated cheese may be sprinkled on top if desired before baking at 220° C (425° F) for 25-30 minutes.
Remove from the oven and cool on a wire rack.

Makes about 2 dozen.

BANANA RICE BISCUITS

Our first version of these biscuits were just out of the oven in time for a morning tea with our finance consultant and his wife. Unfortunately they were so rubbery we all decided they would be better for playing draughts with. This final version is a cracker.

2 cups of brown rice flour
2 mashed bananas
1 tbsp honey
2 tbsps unrefined sesame seed oil
about 1/2 cup of water

Mix all the ingredients well with enough water to make a stiff, sticky batter. Drop dessertspoonfuls of batter on a baking tray dusted with rice flour. Flatten the tops with a wet fork.

Bake at 175° C (350° F) for about 30 minutes until lightly browned.Cool on a wire rack.

Makes about 20 biscuits.

ALMOND TOES
A rich flavoursome shortbread.

2 cups of brown rice flour
2 cups of almond butter
1/4 cup of honey or rice malt
1/4 cup of water

A substitute for almond butter is:
1 1/2 cups of finely chopped or minced almonds
1/2 cup unrefined sunflower oil

Mix everything thoroughly together. Press the mixture out onto a baking tray dusted with rice flour, to a thickness of about 1cm. Cut with a wet knife into little toes and bake at 190°C (375°F) for 30 minutes. Remove from the oven and cool well before transferring the biscuits from the tray.

Makes about 10 big toes (or 20 little ones).

RYE

Description

Rye is a cereal grass similar to wheat. It is a cross-pollinated grass, the hardiest of all the cereals. Rye will survive winter conditions that are too hard for wheat and will thrive on a wide range of soil types. It is particularly suited to poorer soils. Although there are different varieties, rye tends to have longer thinner grains than wheat with a blue-green colour to it.

The rye plant is susceptible to infection by a fungus called ergot. If affected grain is milled, baked and consumed the fungus causes a sickness producing hallucinations, madness and death. It is suspected that many of the plagues during the Middle Ages were caused by ergot poisoning and the strange behaviour associated with it formed an important part of the history of witchcraft.

History

Rye is a relatively new food source for man. Rye originally grew wild in the areas around the Caspian Sea. The earliest evidence of domesticated rye in these areas and in northern Europe dates back to 300 BC. The Romans were among the first to plant rye as a crop. They introduced it to some of their territories during the late stages of the Roman Empire. By the Middle Ages rye was a staple grain throughout Europe. Even today rye is the main grain used for bread in Scandanavia and Eastern Europe.

In England during the Middle Ages a traditional loaf was made from either rye flour or a coarse-ground rye/barley mix called *meslin*. Even as late as the eigtheenth century breads were generally at least 30% rye. Although rye was grown commercially in the north of England it was also regularly imported during this period from Germany and Poland.

Early Dutch settlers took rye to America and developed it as a commercial crop. By the mid nineteenth century thousands of acres of rye were being grown. Rye whiskey is now a major export from America and the industry is one of the largest consumers of rye.

Uses and preparation

Although rye flour contains less gluten than wheat flour and produces a heavier loaf this is well compensated for by the rich flavour, the attractive colour and the good source of protein, vitamins and minerals. Sprouted rye is sweet and delicious, with high protein, B vitamins and vitamin E. Rye can be grown as a grass for juicing or for salads.

Rye is commonly used to make a malt and malt flour for rye beers as well as rye whiskey. It is also flaked as a breakfast cereal, used as a main constituent in adhesives and as a stock food. However for human consumption it is traditionally milled into flours, meals and cracked or kibbled grains. Ten per cent rye flour is often added to commercial wheat flour biscuit and cracker recipes as it improves the quality.

Sourdough ryebreads are leavened with a naturally grown yeast starter. Rye flour is particlarly suited to sourdough leavening. The sourdough not only gives the bread a distinctive sharp flavour but the long rising time and the action of the yeast makes the rye flour more easily digested. Sourdough breads are a tradition throughout northern Europe.

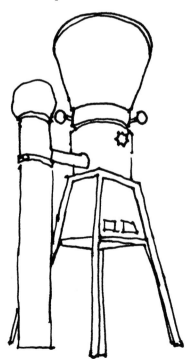

RYE AND PEANUT PORRIDGE
Try this for breakfast served with fresh goat's milk on a crisp clear winter's morning.

1 cup of kibbled rye
1/2 cup of peanut butter (preferably raw)
1/2 cup of raisins
2 tsps honey
1 tbsp sesame seeds
1 tbsp chopped sunflower seeds
2 cups of water

Toast the kibbled rye and the sesame seeds in a dry pan until lightly brown. Bring the water to the boil in a saucepan and add the kibbled rye and sesame seeds. Stir in the peanut butter and raisins and cook for 10-15 minutes. Remove from the heat, add the honey and sunflower seeds and serve.

Makes enough for 3.

RYE SPROUT TOMATO SALAD (Raw)
This salad is a superb filling for pitta bread (see page 22). Stuff some shredded spinach into the bottom of the pocket and top up with salad.

1 cup of minced rye sprouts
6 sliced tomatoes
2 tbsps finely chopped fresh sage
1/4 cup of unrefined cold pressed olive oil
juice from one lemon
shredded spinach

Mix the ingredients together lightly. Chill before serving on a bed of shredded spinach.

Serves 2-4.

RYE-TOFU PÂTÉ(Raw)

1 cup of sprouted rye
1 250g block of firm tofu
4 chopped spring onions
1/2 cup of chopped parsley
1 finely chopped green pepper
1/4 cup of unrefined cold pressed olive oil
1/4 cup of lemon juice
1/4 tsp of garam marsala
1/2 tsp of curry powder

Mash the tofu and mince the sprouted rye. Mix the lemon juice, olive oil and spices well with the tofu-rye mixture and the chopped vegetables. Press the mixture into a mould and chill.

Turn out onto a plate and serve in slices on a bed of fresh shredded lettuce or spinach with a garnish of parsley, a slice of orange and a sprinkle of paprika.

Serves 4.

EYEBALL RYEBALLS

1/2 cup of rye flour
1/3 cup of chopped cashew nuts
1/2 cup muscatel raisins
1/3 cup of grated fresh coconut (or desiccated coconut)
1 tbsp honey
2 tbsps of unrefined cold pressed sesame seed oil
1/2 tsp of natural vanilla essence
water

Mix the ingredients together by hand, adding enough water so they hold together, and shape into balls about 3cm in diameter. The balls may be rolled in some fine shredded coconut for easier handling. Keep cool until serving.

Makes about 8 balls.

STIR FRY RYE
A succulent dish.

1 1/2 cups of rye sprouts
1 chopped onion
1 chopped green pepper
4 sliced tomatoes
1/2 tsp dried sage
1/2 cup of chopped parsley
2 tbsps of cooking oil
soy sauce
unsalted food yeast

Sauté the onion for 2 minutes in the oil, then add the remaining ingredients except the parsley.

Cook on a medium heat for 5-10 minutes then stir in the chopped parsley and serve with seasonings of soy sauce and unsalted food yeast.

Serves 3.

RYE RUSKS

These are delicious wheat-free crispbreads good for teething children and for salad snacks or to accompany soups.

5 cups of rye flour
1/2 cup of unrefined sunflower oil
1 tsp honey
1 cup of warm water
1 cup of soymilk, milk or water
2 tsps of caraway seed
2 tbsps of active dried yeast

Mix the warm water, honey and yeast together and leave for 15 minutes in a warm place to activate. Add the dry ingredients then mix in the oil and enough liquid to form a kneadable dough.

Knead the dough on a floured board for 5-10 minutes. Roll into a log with a diameter of about 10cm. Slice into rounds about 1cm thick and place on an oiled oven tray to rise until doubled in size.

Bake at 205°C (400°F) for about 25 minutes until just browned. Remove from the oven and allow to cool. Split the rounds in two with a sharp knife and bake in a low oven until dry and crisp. Or serve them split, fresh, with a topping of sliced tomato and lettuce.

Makes about 25 rusks.

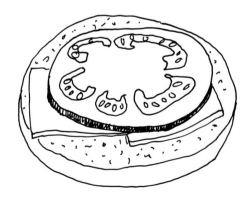

RYE SHORTBREAD

3 cups of whole rye flour
1 cup of unrefined sunflower oil (or 225g of butter)
1/3 cup of honey (or rice malt)

Cream oil and honey thoroughly then beat in the rye flour. Mix well then press the dough out on to a baking tray (or roll between two sheets of greaseproof paper) to a depth of about 1cm.
Bake at 165°C (325°F) for 25 minutes. Cut into bars while still hot.

Makes about 20 pieces.

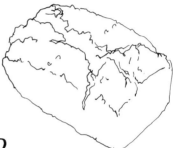

RYE &BARLEY BREAD

A moist flavoursome batter bread that is easy and quick.

2 cups of whole rye flour
2 cups of barley flour
1 cup of warm water
2 tsps of active dried yeast
1 1/2 cups of milk (or warm water)
1/4 cup of unrefined sunflower oil
1 tsp of baking powder (see page 11 for alternative)
1 tsp honey

Stir the yeast and honey into the warm water and leave for 15 minutes in a warm place for the yeast to activate. Mix in the oil, milk, baking powder and the flours. Beat throroughly into a thick batter.
Leave for 15 minutes in a warm place then pour the batter into a well-oiled bread tin. Bake at 175°C (350°F) for 60-80 minutes.

Makes 1 loaf.

WHITEHEART SOURDOUGH RYE BREAD

Our thanks to Gerlinde who introduced us to this Austrian recipe and showed us how to bake it. Over the last few years we have baked thousands of loaves from this recipe and our noses and taste buds still delight in the delicious smell and taste of the bread hot from the oven.

Starter:

2 cups of medium stoneground rye flour

2 1/2 cups of warm water (or water potatoes have been cooked in)

Mix together in a jar and leave in a warm place for about 4 days with a cloth tied over the top of the jar. The natural yeast should turn this batter into a bubbling brew. This starter can now be stored in the refrigerator.

To speed the growth of the bug and to change the flavours of the yeasts 1/2 teaspoon of active dried yeast or 1/2 teaspoon of yogurt can be added.

Remember, when you start to make the bread, to return the same amount of starter from the leavened sponge to restock your bug as you added to the sponge earlier. *It is important to add the spongy batter back to your starter before you add the salt because the salt will kill the natural yeasts.*

The Bread

> 6 cups of medium stoneground rye flour
> 2 tbsps starter
> 3 tbsps caraway seeds
> 1 cup of water
> 1/2 tsp of salt

Mix 4 cups of flour with the starter, caraway seeds and water. Beat well into a batter. Leave this to rise into a sponge for 12-18 hours. Not only does this give the natural yeasts a chance to grow through the batter but the long soaking makes the rye much more digestible.

Now add 2 tbsps of the sponge back to your starter jar.

Mix in the remaining flour and the salt. Stir for about 10 minutes into a stiff sticky mud.

Oil 2 bread tins well and sprinkle some wholegrain rolled oats evenly in the tins for decoration. Spoon in this grey, muddy dough until the tins are about 3/4 full. Press the sticky mixture well into the corners of the tin. Smooth the top with wet fingers and slash cross hatching deeply with a sharp wet knife to let the steam out. (If you don't cut deep enough the loaf erupts into mountains and cliffs.). We found the easiest way to handle this dough is to keep your hands wet, then it seems to stick less.

Bake at 230° C (450° F) for 20 minutes, then turn the heat down to 150° C (300° F) and bake for another 50 minutes. Remove from the tin and leave to cool on a wire rack. A great variation is the addition of 1/2 cup of fresh chopped herbs.

Makes 2 loaves.

HEAVY FRUIT RYE BREAD
A hearty German-style fruit bread which keeps for weeks.

2 cups of stoneground rye flour
3 tbsps soy flour
1 tbsp active dried yeast
1 cup of warm water
1/3 cup of unrefined sunflower oil
1/2 cup of honey
3 cups of chopped mixed dried fruit
1 cup of mixed chopped nuts (or more fruit)

Mix the yeast and honey in the warm water and leave for 15 minutes in a warm place to rise. Stir the remaining ingredients in thoroughly and leave for 10-15 minutes.

Knead the dough for about 5 minutes, on a well floured board, into a moist dough.

Put into an oiled bread tin and leave to rise in a warm place for about 60 minutes until doubled in size. Bake at 160°C (325°F) for 50 minutes.

Makes 1 big fruity cake.

TRITICALE

Description

Triticale is a very recent addition to the food crops of man. It is a manmade hybrid grain achieved by crossing varieties of wheat and rye. The aim was to produce a grass with the hardiness of rye and the yield of wheat which had a high protein and baked like a wheat. The resulting grain fits the prescription very well. Triticale is higher in protein than either wheat or rye and the crop yields well even in poorer soils.

The name *Triticale* is derived from the Latin name for wheat *Triticum* and Rye, *Secale*. It is pronounced *Trit-i-car-lee.*

History

The first fertile wheat/rye crosses were bred in Sweden in the 1930's. Although these plants were able to reproduce it has taken considerable research, trials and variety selection to produce plants with commercial potential.

The two main centres for research and development of Triticale are in Mexico and Canada. They have improved the proportion of the amino acid lysine, from the rye plant, and adapted strains for different conditions. Trials are still under way in most countries to establish suitable varieties for different conditions.

Uses and Preparation

Triticale flour has a sweet rye-like flavour but bakes more like wheat flour than rye.It has a light, soft gluten that requires much less work to turn into a good dough. Even so commercial triticale loaves generally have up to 60% wheat flour added to improve the elasticity of the dough.

Chapatis and flatbreads are successful with triticale flour but again the quality is improved with the addition of up to 40% wheat flour or up to 20% chickpea flour. Chickpea flour also raises the nutritive value.

Triticale is most suitable for biscuits, cakes, pancakes and waffles where the rye flavour can be enjoyed and the gluten quality is not important.

Sprouted triticale resembles wheat but is lighter in colour. The sprouts are sweet and flavoursome. Triticale sprouts are the most tender of all the sprouted cereals. The grain sprouts quickly and easily yielding a protein content twice that of rye with higher amounts of essential amino acids than wheat.

Triticale flour can generally be used as a substitute for rye flour, or as a 50/50 blend with wheat flour in yeasted wheat flour recipes, biscuits and pancake recipes. The flour is suitable for thickening sauces, making crumble toppings and piecrusts. People with allergies to wheat but not rye may be able to tolerate triticale flour but try a little first before you eat a big triticale bread sandwich.

HOT SPROUT BREAKFAST

1/2 cup of minced triticale sprouts
1/2 cup of oatmeal (or kibbled buckwheat)
1/2 cup of chopped dates
2 cups of water
chopped nuts

Mix the ingredients together in a saucepan and bring to the boil stirring constantly. Simmer on a low heat for 10-15 minutes until the cereal is cooked.

Serve with yogurt, cream or soymilk and a sprinkling of chopped nuts.

Makes a breakfast for 2.

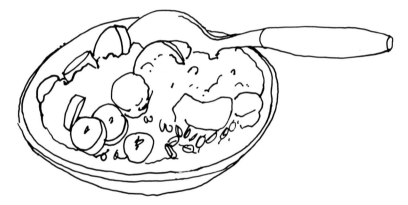

SUPERBALE TRITICALE (Raw)

1 cup of triticale sprouts
2 tbsps of liquid honey
3 tbsps grated fresh coconut
1/2 cup of chopped fresh fruit
1 cup of chilled yogurt

Mix the ingredients together and serve.

Makes a delicious appetiser or breakfast for 2.

TRITICALE LENTIL PILAF

This pilaf is delicious and well-presented on a bed of shredded spinach with a garnish of parsley and a twist of sliced orange.

1/2 cup of whole triticale
1/2 cup of brown lentils
1 chopped onion
1/2 cup of sliced carrots
1/2 cup of sliced celery
1 tbsp of cooking oil
1/4 tsp of ground cardamom
1/2 tsp of mixed herbs
2 cups of vegetable stock

Bring the triticale to the boil in a pot of water. After 25 minutes add the lentils and boil for another 15 minutes until both are cooked. Drain and reserve the liquid for stock.

Lightly sauté the onions, carrots and celery in the oil for 2 minutes, then stir in the cooked triticale and lentils. Add the herbs and stock. Cover and steam for 10 minutes before serving.

Serves 4.

TRITICALE BUMBLEBEES (Raw)

A rich after dinner top-off.

1 cup of sprouted triticale
1 cup of cashew pieces
1 cup of chopped figs
1/2 cup of cream cheese (optional)
1/2 cup of rice flour or sesame seeds

Mince the ingredients together and form into 3cm balls. Roll them in the rice flour or sesame seeds. Chill then serve.

Makes about 12.

50

TRITICALE FRESH FRUIT PIE

Shell
> 1 1/2 cups of triticale flour
> 1/2 cup of unrefined sunflower oil
> about 1/2 cup of water

Filling
> 6 cups of fresh strawberries, peaches (and/or other fruit)
> 1/4 cup of honey
> 1 cup of cream or soycream

Mix the oil and the flour thoroughly, until it looks like even crumbs. Sprinkle the water on gradually, mixing it in as you go, until the mixture forms a cohesive soft dough.

Roll the dough out on a floured board into a circle just larger than the piedish. Transfer the dough to the piedish by wrapping it around the rolling pin. Trim the edges and press into the piedish.

Prick the pastry evenly all over with a fork, fill with one layer of dried beans (to keep the bottom flat) and fully bake at 215° C (425° F) for 20 minutes until the crust is lightly browned. Remove from the oven and allow to cool.

Chop the fruit roughly and stir with the honey. Chill. To serve pour the chilled fruit into the pie shell, whip the cream and spread over the fruit.

Serves 4-6.

TRITICALE SHORTBREAD

1 1/2 cups of triticale flour
1 1/2 cups of brown rice flour
1 cup of unrefined sunflower oil (or 225g of butter)
1/3 cup of honey or rice malt

Beat the honey and oil together well. Mix with the flours to make a firm dough.

Roll out the dough to a thickness of about 1cm. Place on an oiled baking tray and cut into biscuit sized pieces with a knife. Prick each piece several times with a fork.

Bake at 150°C (300°F) for 45-50 minutes.

Makes about 20 pieces.

COCONUT BISCUITS

1 cup of triticale flour
1/2 cup of honey
3 cups of desiccated coconut
juice from 1 orange
grated peel from one orange
1/4 cup of water

Mix the ingredients together thoroughly and knead well. Form into 3cm balls and place on an oiled baking tray. Press down gently with a wet fork.

Bake for 25-30 minutes at 180°C (350°F).

Makes about 15.

TRITICALE DATE SLICE

1 cup of triticale flour
1 cup of rolled oats
1 cup of fine shredded coconut
1/2 tsp of ground mixed spice
250g of butter
2 tbsps of honey
1 cup of chopped dates or prunes
2 cups of water
1/2 tsp of natural vanilla essence

Melt the butter with the honey and then mix with the flour, oats, coconut and spice. Press half this mixture into an oiled biscuit tray to a thickness of about 1 cm.
Simmer the dates with the water and vanilla essence until soft. Drain off excess liquid, mash and spread over the base. Press the remaining half of the base mixture over the top of the date paste.
Bake at 205°C (400°F) for 15-20 minutes until lightly browned, remove from the oven and leave in the tin until cool.

Makes about 10 slices.

RAW BANANA BREAD (Raw)

1/2 cup of sprouted triticale
1 cup of triticale flour
1 mashed banana
2 tsps of honey
1/4 tsp natural vanilla essence
chopped nuts

Mince the triticale sprouts finely and combine with the other ingredients to form a dough that is not sticky.
Roll the dough into a log, roll the log in the chopped nuts and wrap in greaseproof paper. Chill overnight then serve sliced thinly.

Makes 1 log.

NO KNEAD TRITICALE BREAD
Makes lovely toast - delicious flavour.

6 cups of triticale flour
2 tbsps active dried yeast
1 tsp molasses
2 tsps honey or rice malt
about 3 cups of warm water

Dissolve the yeast, honey and molasses in 2 cups of the warm water and leave to rise for 15 minutes in a warm place. Add this mixture to the flour, mixing it thoroughly into a sticky dough. Add as much of the third cup of water as necessary (water absorption is often variable with wholemeal flours). Tip the sticky dough into two well-oiled bread tins and let rise for 1 hour in a warm place.

Bake at 205°C (400°F) for about 40 minutes until the crust is brown. De-tin the loaves onto wire racks.

Makes 2 loaves.

BUCKWHEAT

Description

Buckwheat is the seed from a herbaceous plant belonging to the rhubarb family and is not a wheat or even a cereal grain. The plants are red and green bushes with heart-shaped leaves. In mid-summer they flower with several heads of pinky white blooms from which the seeds form.

The soft pyramid-shaped seeds or groats are encased in a tough dark brown, indigestible sheath.

Buckwheat is popular with growers as it is very hardy and matures more quickly than the cereal grains. It can thus be used to oversow early crops that have failed. However the yield is much lower than most other grain crops and the birds enjoy the ripe seeds.

Although buckwheat is not strictly a grain and has no gluten, it does have a constituent, called a gluten analogue, which behaves in a similar way to grain glutens. Many people allergic to grain gluten can tolerate buckwheat and its byproducts comfortably.

History

Buckwheat originated in Central and North East Asia and has been a traditional food of the Russians, the Mongols and the northern Chinese. Although well known and popular in these areas, buckwheat has been commercially grown and harvested only recently in other countries.

The Tartars first introduced buckwheat to Europe and it was cultivated in Germany from the fifteenth century.

The seed is traditionally roasted before use. The roasted seed or *kasha* is a traditional Russian food but is also popular throughout northern Europe as a substitute for potatoes, rice or other grains. *Kasha* may be served in the classic way with cabbage, black bread and sour cream, or made into a pilaf with stock and onions. The Russians also use buckwheat flour to make tiny paper-thin pancakes called *blini*.

The Japanese hold a special place for buckwheat in their

culture. Not only is *soba* (buckwheat noodles) a popular traditional food but the hulls have long been used as a filling for cushions and pillows.

The increase in popularity and availability of buckwheat over the last fifty years is largely attributable to the move to healthier foods which values buckwheat as a replacement for wheat.

Uses and Preparation

Buckwheat has a balance of proteins that makes it nutritionally better than the cereal grains. This is due to the higher proportion of the amino acid, lysine. It is also high in iron and B vitamins.

The seeds can be sprouted and the young plants used in salads and for juicing. However the most common use of the seed is for the hulls to be removed and the groats used either whole, kibbled or milled into flour.

Traditionally, perhaps due to the difficulties of winnowing, a proportion of hulls was milled with the groats giving a gray colour to the flour and a slightly bitter flavour. We feel this is unnecessary today with modern sieving techniques. The hulls are not digestible and their inclusion in the flour reduces its baking quality and flavour.

The flour bakes excellently and is comparable to brown rice flour. Biscuits brown well and the flour makes excellent sauces.

One of the most useful qualities of buckwheat flour is its ability to act as a binder in breads, biscuits, cakes, pancakes and fritters. It is not as effective as a full gluten wheat flour but can give very satisfying results.

BUCKWHEAT PORRIDGE

There are many variations of buckwheat porridge recipes . Here are two of our favourites.

1. 1 1/2 cups of buckwheat groats
    2 1/2 cups of boiling water
    1/3 cup of raisins

    Stir the groats into boiling water in a large saucepan and cook for about 20 minutes until soft. Add the raisins and cook another 5 minutes. Sweeten with honey and serve with soymilk or yogurt.

    Serves 3.

2. 1 cup of buckwheat groats
    3 cups of rice flakes
    1/2 cup of rice bran
    1/2 cup of cracked millet
    honey or rice malt

    Mix the dry ingredients together and store in an airtight tin. For each serving mix 1/2 cup of the mixture with 1 1/2 cups of water.
    Stir over a medium heat and cook for 15 minutes. Stir in 1 teaspoon of sweetening and serve.
    Chopped fresh and dried fruit can be added to these porridges for a special start to the day.

    Serves 5-6.

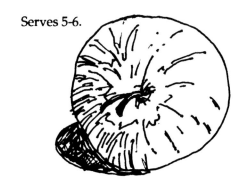

BUCKWHEAT-BARLEY PANCAKES

1 cup of buckwheat flour
2 cups of barley flour
1 tbsp of active dried yeast
1 cup of warm water
1/2 cup of soymilk (or water)
1/4 cup of unrefined sunflower oil
2 tbsps of honey

Mix yeast and honey with the warm water and the soymilk. Leave to rise for 20 minutes.

Whisk in the barley flour, buckwheat flour and the oil to form a smooth batter. For each pancake pour about 1/4 cup of batter into a hot, lightly oiled pan. Cook for about 2 minutes then turn the pancake and cook for another 2 minutes after bubbles form on the surface.

Makes 12 pancakes.

BUCKWHEAT GREENS (Raw)
A delicious salad green, full of vitamins and minerals.

1 cup of unhulled buckwheat

Soak the whole buckwheat in a jar for 8 hours then plant in a seed tray with a covering of potting mix. Grow the plants for 2-3 weeks before trimming them with scissors as for cress and wheatgrass, for use in salads, sandwiches and stews.

The tender young plants can also be pulled out, washed and used whole. They are particularly rich in chlorophyll, calcium and lecithin.

BUCKWHEAT GROATS SALAD (Raw)

2 cups of buckwheat groats
2 cups of tomato juice
1 cup of chopped celery
1 cup of chopped green pepper
1 cup of sprouted aduki beans
2 sliced spring onions
1 finely chopped clove of garlic
1 small shredded lettuce
1 cup of plain unsweetened yogurt
3 tsps of chopped fresh basil

Soak the groats in the tomato juice overnight or until the juice is absorbed.

Mix in the yogurt then add the remaining ingredients. Toss lightly. Serve on a bed of steamed brown rice.

Serves 2-3.

BUCKWHEAT CABBAGE ROLLS

2 cups of buckwheat groats
1 chopped onion
1 chopped green pepper
1/4 cup of chopped sunflower seeds
1/2 cup of chopped peanuts
3 tbsps of unrefined olive oil
4 cups of boiling water
1 cabbage
soy sauce
unsalted food yeast

Sauté the onion and green pepper for 2 minutes then add the buckwheat groats. Cook for a further 2 minutes then add the boiling water and simmer for 15 minutes until soft. Add the chopped peanuts and sunflower seeds. Season with yeast and soy sauce.

Core the cabbage and steam the leaves until pliable. Separate the leaves and place 2 heaped tablespoons of the groat mixture on each leaf. Roll them up, tucking in the sides.

Place the cabbage rolls in an oiled baking dish. Pour warm water over the rolls so the dish is half full. Cover and bake at 175°C (350°F) for 50-60 minutes.

Serve with a spicy sauce and salads.

Makes 8 large rolls.

KASHA
This traditonal Russian dish has a unique flavour and texture.

1 cup of toasted buckwheat groats
1 chopped onion
2 tbsps of butter (or unrefined sunflower oil)
1 cup of water

Cook the onion lightly in the butter and mix in the buckwheat groats. Add the water, bring to the boil then turn down heat and simmer for 10-15 minutes.

Serves 2.

BUCKWHEAT-CORN FRITTERS

2 cups of buckwheat flour
2 cups of cooked sweetcorn
1 finely chopped onion
1 1/2 cups of soymilk (or milk)
1 tsp of dried basil
1/2 cup of fresh chopped parsley
soy sauce
unsalted food yeast
kelp powder

Mix the ingredients thoroughly to form a stiff mixture. Add the soy sauce, unsalted food yeast and kelp powder to season.
Drop gently, by the tablespoonful, into a medium-hot pan with a small amount of oil in it. Fry on both sides for 2-3 minutes until cooked.
Serve with raw tomato sauce, or chutney, and salad. See recipes on pages 23 and 79.

Makes 12 fritters.

BUCKWHEAT SOBA

Simple, delightful, fresh nutritious noodles from a traditional Japanese recipe.

1 cup of buckwheat flour
1 tbsp unrefined soya bean oil
1/3 cup of water
salt (optional)
oil

Combine all the ingredients to form a firm dough. Knead for 10 minutes. Place on an oiled tray and roll as thinly as possible. Slice into fine strips.

Bring a large pot of water to the boil (add salt if desired). Add another 2 tsps of oil to the water to prevent the noodles from sticking together. Boil the noodles for 3 minutes. Drain and serve.

Serves 2.

GINGERBREAD PEOPLE

2 cups of buckwheat flour
2 tsps powdered ginger
1/4 cup of honey
1 tsp baking powder
1/4 cup unrefined sunflower oil
2 tbsps molasses
1/4 cup of water
currants
long thread coconut
dried peel

Mix together the dry ingredients. Separately mix the oil, honey, molasses and water. Stir this into the flour with enough water to form a firm dough.

Roll out the dough on a floured board or between two sheets of greaseproof paper. With a sharp knife, or pattern cutter, cut out the shapes for 6 gingerbread people.

Use the currants for eyes, the long thread coconut for hair and a piece of dried peel for the mouth. Belts, buttons and bows can be made from left over strips of dough. Shape the dough pieces, then moisten and press onto the gingerbread body.

Bake at 175° C (350° F) for about 10 minutes until the gingerbread people are firm and starting to brown at the edges. Remove carefully from the oven and cool.

Makes about 6 well-dressed gingerbread people.

BASIC BUCKWHEAT BISCUITS
Real buckwheat flavoured crackers for dips and snacks.

1 cup of buckwheat flour
2 tbsps of unrefined sesame seed oil
water
pinch of salt (optional)

Mix the ingredients together and add enough water to make a firm dough. Roll out very thin and cut into 5cm squares.

Bake on an oiled baking tray at 175° C (350° F) for 20-30 minutes.

To this basic recipe try adding herbs and a dash of curry powder for savoury biscuits or a teaspoon of honey or rice malt and some cinnamon or other spices for sweeter biscuits.

Makes about 10.

BUCKWHEAT KASHA BREAD

1 cup of buckwheat flour
1/2 cup buckwheat groats
1 1/2 cups of extra-fine wholemeal flour
1/4 cup of wheatgerm
1/3 cup of molasses
1 tbsp honey
1 tbsp active dried yeast
1/4 cup of butter or unrefined sunflower oil
1/2 tsp of cinnamon
1 cup of warm water

Boil the buckwheat groats for about 20 minutes until cooked.
Mix the yeast, honey and molasses with the warm water in a large
mixing bowl and leave to activate for about 15 minutes.

Drain and cool the buckwheat groats then add them to the
yeast mixture with the remaining ingredients.

Mix together thoroughly for about 10 minutes. Cover with a
towel and put in a warm place to rise for 1 hour. Stir the dough
down and put in a large oiled bread tin. Let rise for 1 more hour in
a warm place.

Bake at 200° C (390 ° F) for 45 minutes. Remove from oven,
de-tin and cool on a rack.

Makes 1 rich brown loaf.

MILLET

Description

Millet is a cereal grain that thrives in hot dry conditions. The grain is small and round, encased in an indigestible pale yellow hull. It has a short growing season and, under suitable conditions, two crops a year can be planted and harvested.

Sorghum is a member of the millet family.It has larger seeds than millet although nutritionally it is very similar. It is a common crop in Africa where its drought resistant qualities have ensured its survival for centuries. In drought conditions the plants stop growing, as if dormant, but do not die. When rain comes the plants start growing again.

High quality organic and biodynamically grown millet is grown in Australia, Canada and America.

History

Millet is probably the oldest food source of man. Evidence suggests varieties of millet were first domesticated in pre-historic times. Swiss stone-age cave dwellers grew the variety we have named *proso*. Finger millet, *ragi*, was cultivated during the same pre-historic times in India and Central Africa.

Over 10,000 years ago in China the foxtail millet was the staple food before the introduction of rice. The Chinese made a thin flatbread from ground millet flour. Several thousand years later millet formed part of the diet of the Ancient Romans. They had a traditional dish similar to a millet porridge.

These varieties and newer strains are still a staple food in many parts of Africa, Asia, Central America and the Middle East.

Uses and Preparation

Millet is one of the most nutritious and digestible grains. It is high in B vitamins with good proportions of calcium and iron. It is also comparatively high in protein.The hard outer hull needs to be removed before milling as it is not suitable for our stomach lining. However the whole millet sprouts successfully and is a great addition to salads, sandwiches and soups.

Hulled millet is cooked as it is for savoury or breakfast cereal dishes. It is also milled into cracked millet, millet meal and fine millet flour.

Traditionally the millets are eaten either whole or as a meal for porridges and flatbreads. A large proportion of harvested millet is used to make beverages.

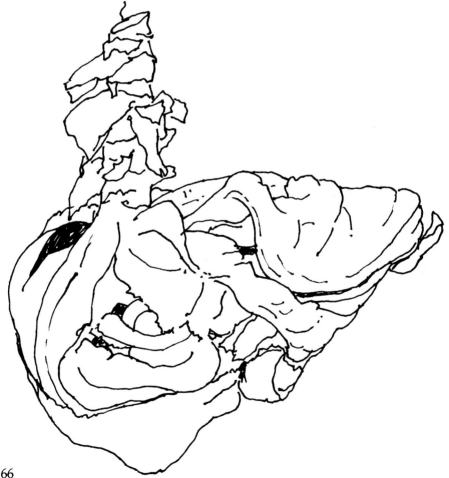

MILLET PORRIDGE

1/2 cup of hulled millet
2 cups of soymilk (milk, goat's milk or water)
1 grated apple
1/2 cup of raisins or dates

Bring the millet to the boil in the milk then reduce the heat and simmer for about 25 minutes until cooked. Stir in the fruit and serve.

Serves 2.

ALMOND-MILLET TOFU LOG (Raw)
Millet sprouts are ideal for dessert dishes, being sweet and chewy with a nutty flavour. They are at their best when the shoot has just appeared.

1/2 cup of sprouted millet seeds
1 300g block of soft tofu
1/2 cup of chopped raisins
1/3 cup of ground almonds
1/2 cup of flaked almonds
1/3 cup of chopped pistachio nuts
2 tbsps of grated orange rind
1/2 cup of mashed banana
1/4 tsp ground nutmeg
1/4 tsp ground mace

Stir the tofu into a paste with the ground almonds, mashed banana and spices. Apart from the flaked almonds add the remaining ingredients and mix together.

Spoon this mixture onto a piece of foil and roll it up into a log. Chill for about 3 hours. Remove the foil and roll the log in the flaked almonds. Serve in slices.

Makes 1 log.

FRESH HERB MILLET SALAD

1 cup of cooked hulled millet
1 cup of chopped fresh parsley
1/2 cup of chopped fresh watercress
1 tbsp of chopped fresh dill or fennel
1/2 cup of chopped spring onions
1 tbsp of unrefined cold pressed olive oil
juice of one lemon

Mix the ingredients lightly together. Chill and serve.

Makes enough for 3-4.

MIKE McCAMMONS MILLET

A naturopath friend of mine advised a course of cleansing for me after I had severe back pain several years ago. Millet and garlic were two of the staples of the prescribed diet. This dish became a nightly event for many weeks. (And my back has never been better.)

1 cup of hulled millet
1/4 cup of unrefined sesame seed oil
1 chopped onion
2 chopped cloves of garlic (or more)
4 cups of water
1/2 cup of chopped parsley
1/3 cup of unsalted food yeast

Sauté the millet, onion and garlic in the oil for 2-3 minutes. Add the water and simmer for 20-30 minutes until cooked. Before serving stir in the food yeast and parsley.

Makes enough for 4.

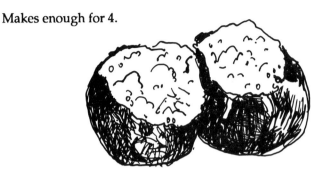

MILLET STUFFING
FOR PEPPERS AND TOMATOES

A delight for those who like their cooked food with a bit of life in it.

1 cup of hulled or cracked millet
8 green or red peppers, or tomatoes
1 chopped onion
2 tbsps of chopped parsley
1/2 cup of sliced mushrooms
1 tsp of chopped fresh basil
1 cup of tomato sauce (homemade is best)
1/2 cup of grated cheese (optional)

Wash and cut the tops off the peppers or tomatoes. Carefully dig out the insides. The pepper seeds can be discarded but the tomato pulp can be added to the stuffing mixture.

Boil the millet until cooked and sauté the chopped onion in a little oil for a few minutes. Add the onion to the millet along with the herbs, mushrooms and tomato sauce.

Spoon the filling into the pepper or tomato shells. Stack into a breadtin and cover with grated cheese. Bake at 175°C (350°F) for about 15 minutes.

Serves 4.

SAVOURY CRACKERS

1 cup of hulled or cracked millet
2 cups of water
1 cup of buckwheat flour
1 tsp of curry powder
1/2 cup of finely chopped onion
paprika

Simmer the millet and onion in the water for about 15 minutes until the water is absorbed. Stir in the buckwheat flour and curry powder and mix well. Flour a baking tray with buckwheat or millet flour and press the mixture out to a depth of about 1 cm. Slice it into biscuit-size strips with a wet knife and sprinkle with paprika.
Bake at 175° C (350° F) for 30-40 minutes.

Makes about 15.

VEGE TOFU CURRY ON MILLET

4 cups of hot, cooked millet (1 1/2 cups raw)
1 chopped green pepper
5 cups of chopped mixed vegetables
1 cup of diced tofu
1 sliced onion
1 clove of minced garlic
1 tsp of grated ginger
1 cup of raw peanuts and cashews
1/2 cup of raisins
1 1/2 cups of vege stock
4 tbsps of cooking oil
1 tsp of ground cumin
1/2 tsp of coriander
1/2 tsp of ground cloves
1/2 tsp of chilli powder
1 tsp of turmeric
3 tsps of curry powder

Heat the oil in a pan, over a low heat, and sauté the spices with the garlic, onion and ginger for about 10 minutes. Add the tofu, nuts, raisins and green pepper and cook for a further 10 minutes stirring frequently.

Stir in the vegetables and stock, cover, and simmer for another 10 minutes.

Spoon the cooked hot millet onto warmed plates making a nest in the middle. Spoon the curried vegetables over the millet and serve immediately.

Serves 4.

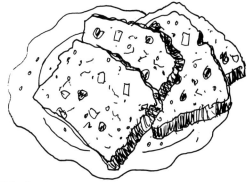

COELIAC FRUIT CAKE
Haute Cuisine, a lovely crunchy texture and very filling.

1/2 cup of millet flour
1/2 cup of cracked millet
1 cup of brown rice flour
1/2 cup of ground (or well chopped) sunflower seeds
2 cups of water or fruit juice
2 cups of chopped dried fruit
1/2 cup of tahini (sesame seed butter)

Simmer fruit, liquid and tahini for 2 minutes. Mix this with the dry ingredients and beat well, into a thick batter. Pour this mixture into an oiled bread tin and bake at 175°C (350°F) for about 60 minutes until the cake goes brown on top.

Let the cake cool for 10 minutes in the tin. Ease the cake out onto a wire rack and leave to cool completely before eating.

Makes 1 loaf.

MILLET BANANA CAKE

1/2 cup of fine millet flour
2 tsp cinnamon
1 cup of mashed banana
1 cup of ground or finely chopped sunflower seeds
1/2 cup of arrowroot powder
1/4 cup of honey
2 tsp baking powder (see alternative on page 11)
1/4 tsp pure vanilla essence
1/3 cup of water

Mix the flour, spices, sunflower seeds, arrowroot and baking powder together in a bowl. Beat the remaining ingredients in to form a thick batter.

Pour the mixture into an oiled cake tin. Bake for about 70 minutes at 165° C (325° F). Remove from oven and cover while cooling to retain moisture.

Makes 1 loaf.

MILLET MUFFINS

1 1/2 cups of fine millet flour
1 1/2 cups of fine rice flour
2 mashed bananas
1 tsp of baking powder (see alternative on page 11)
1/4 cup of unrefined sunflower oil
1/2 cup of mixed dried fruit
about 1 cup of soymilk (or milk, or water)

Mix the flours and the baking powder. Add the remaining ingredients and beat the mixture into a thick batter.

Spoon into an oiled muffin tray. Bake at 175°C (350°F) for 25-30 minutes.

Makes 12.

MILLET BREAD

1 cup of cracked millet or millet meal
1 cup of millet flour
2 cups of triticale flour (or more wholemeal)
3 cups of extra-fine wholemeal flour
3 cups of wholemeal flour
1 cup of soy flour
2 1/2 cups of warm water
1 tbsp active dried yeast
1/4 cup of molasses
1/4 cup of unrefined sesame oil
3 tbsps sesame seeds
1/2 tsp salt (optional)

Dissolve the yeast in a large bread bowl with the warm water and molasses. Add the wholemeal flour a cup at a time, stirring in well before adding the next cup. Beat for 5-10 minutes into a thick batter. Cover the bowl and leave in a warm place for 60 minutes to rise.

Mix in the remaining ingredients except the sesame seeds. As soon as the mixture forms a workable dough tip it out of the bowl and knead it on a floured board for at least 10 minutes. Brush the dough with oil and leave to rise, in a covered bowl, in a warm place for 50 minutes. Press the dough down and leave to rise for a further 45 minutes. The dough should be much lighter this time.

Tip 2 tablespoons of the sesame seeds into oiled bread tins and shake the tins around so the seeds stick evenly to the sides.Shape the dough into loaves and place in the bread tins. Brush the tops with oil and scatter the 3rd tablespoon of sesame seeds over them.

Leave the dough to rise in the tins in a warm place for 20-30 minutes. Bake at 175° C (350° F) for 50-60 minutes. Remove from the oven, de-tin and cool on a wire rack.

Makes 2 loaves.

GINGER APPLE MUFFINS

1 1/2 cups of millet flour
1 1/2 cups of brown rice flour
1/4 cup of soft tofu
1/4 cup of unrefined sunflower oil
1 1/2 cups of warm water
1 tsp of ground cloves
1 cup of cooked apple
2 tsps of ground ginger
2 tsps of baking powder (see alternative on page 11)

Mix all the ingredients into a thick batter and beat well. Spoon into a well oiled muffin tray.

Preheat the oven to 205° C (400° F) and bake for 30-35 minutes.

Makes 12.

BARLEY

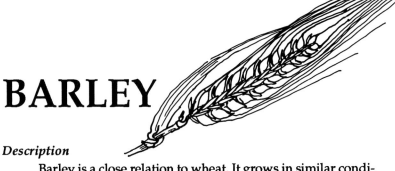

Description

Barley is a close relation to wheat. It grows in similar conditions and climates. An important difference is the characteristic way the barley husks grow firmly attached to the grain kernel. This indigestible outer layer cannot be threshed off as with wheat. The husk is removed by an abrasive process known as 'pearling'.

Lightly rubbed barley is known as 'pot barley'; it has most of the bran and nutrients intact (and has a full flavour). However the most common form of barley available today for human consumption is 'pearled barley'; which is polished to the inside layer of the grain. Barley contains very little gluten and is unsuitable for light, risen breads and pastries.

History

Barley is one of the oldest food crops of man. Evidence has revealed wild barley was used by nomadic tribes as early as 40,000 BC, but the earliest samples of cultivated barley were found in Eygpt, dating back to about 5000 BC.

From its origins in the Middle East, barley spread throughout the civilised world, becoming the chief food source of the ancient Roman and Greek cultures. Its popularity for human consumption waned from the sixteenth century, when wheat and rye started to be more commonly used.

Barley has been important to the brewing industry as the basis for malt for thousands of years. Today most of the world's barley harvest is used for malting or animal food.

Uses and Preparation

Barley is a nutritionally rich grain but as it is very low in gluten its main uses are for porridges, soups and stews or milled into flour for biscuits, cakes and flatbreads.

Barley sprouts well, as brewers will testify; however only whole barley or 'pot barley' has the germ intact and will sprout. The sprouts are not as sweet as wheat but are delicious in salads or steamed. The sprouts can be roasted and ground for use as a coffee substitute.

Barley flour browns well and makes good sauces.

LEMON BARLEY WATER
This is a variant of the old English recipe favoured to put a blush on the pale cheeks of English women. It is a refreshing and nutritious drink either chilled or hot.

2 1/2 pints of water (1 1/2 litres)
1/2 cup of pearled barley
3 lemons

Simmer the barley in the water, for about an hour, with one lemon sliced into large slices. Strain off the barley and lemon chunks. Cool the remaining liquid. Add the juice from the remaining lemons, mix well and serve with a sprig of mint and crushed ice.

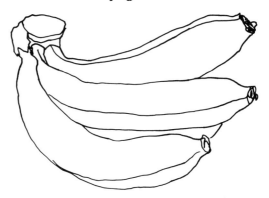

BANANA BARLEY PANCAKES
Serve for breakfast or anytime.

3 cups of barley flour
1 cup of mashed banana
2 1/2 cups of water

Mix the ingredients into a batter. Pour small amounts onto a lightly oiled hot griddle or frying pan.

Flip over after a minute and cook on the other side. Keep the pancakes thin or they get too stodgy. These pancakes are best served with lemon juice and yogurt or whipped cream.

Makes about 10 pancakes.

BARLEY-BUCKWHEAT PANCAKES

2 cups of barley flour
1 cup of buckwheat flour
1 tbsp of active dried yeast
1 cup of warm water
1/2 cup of soymilk (or water)
1/4 cup of unrefined sunflower oil
2 tbsps of honey

Mix yeast and honey into the warm water and the soymilk. Leave to rise for 20 minutes.

Whisk in the barley flour, buckwheat flour and the oil to form a smooth batter. Pour about 1/4 cup of batter into a hot, lightly oiled pan. Cook for about 2 minutes then turn the pancake and cook for another 2 minutes after bubbles form on the surface.

Makes about 8.

AVOCADO BARLEY PANCAKES

A superb, savoury combination. We recommend adding some fresh chopped herbs and serving with raw tomato sauce.

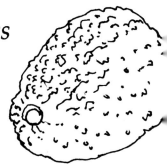

3 cups of barley flour
1 mashed avocado
1 tsp unsalted food yeast
2 1/2 cups of water
2 tsps of mixed chopped fresh herbs

Mix the ingredients into a batter. Pour small amounts onto a lightly oiled medium-hot griddle or frying pan.

Flip over after about 2 minutes and cook on the other side. Keep the pancakes thin or they get too stodgy.

Makes about 10.

SIMPLE RAW TOMATO SAUCE (Raw)
Delicious with pitta bread and savoury pancakes.

4 tomatoes
1 small chopped onion
1 tsp basil
1 pinch of cayenne
1/4 cup of cider vinegar
1 tsp honey

Blend to a sauce and serve.

GEORGIOUS BARLEY SOUP
*From a traditional Russian recipe. A hearty soup that is still light
enough to let you move around afterwards.*

1/2 cup of pearled barley
1 chopped small onion
1 tbsp butter or oil
1/2 cup of vegetable stock or water
1 tbsp of rye flour
1 cup of yogurt
1/4 tsp dill
1/2 tsp coriander
chopped fresh mint
chopped fresh parsley
juice of one small lemon

Boil the barley for about 30 minutes until cooked. Sauté the
onion with the butter in a soup pot for 2-3 minutes. Add the stock,
herbs and cooked barley with any remaining water it was cooked
with. Simmer for 20 minutes.

Mix the flour with the yogurt and lemon juice. Remove soup
from heat. Allow to cool for 5-10 minutes then gradually stir in the
yogurt mixture. Stir in the fresh herbs and serve.

Serves 4.

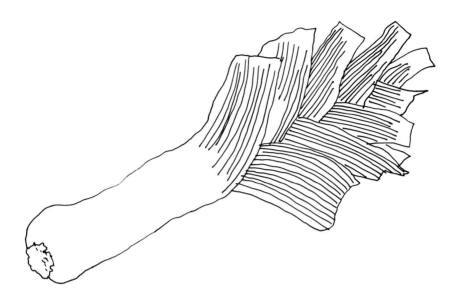

BARLEY BROTH

This could be the very recipe for the broth that kept Rochester warm while he was storming about over the moors. It is at its best served on a cold winter's night with slices of fresh baked bread after you have been out in the rain for hours trying to fix the car.

1 cup of pearled barley
6 cups of vegetable stock
1/2 cup of peas, chopped beans (or other seasonable green vegetable)
1 small turnip
2 carrots
1 leek (or onion)
2 cups of chopped kale (or silverbeet)
1/2 cup of chopped parsley

Dice the turnip and chop the carrots and leek into small pieces. Add these and the other vegetables and the barley to the stock.

Simmer for about 30 minutes then serve with slices of fresh baked bread.

Serves 6.

BARLEY RISSOLES

Yummy, savoury flavour and they really do go golden-brown. Very more-ish.

2 cups of cooked pearled (or pot) barley (1/2 cup raw)
1 chopped tomato
1/2 minced or finely chopped onion
1/2 tsp chopped fresh parsley
1/2 tsp chopped fresh thyme
1/2 cup of pea flour
water
(1/2 cup of grated cheese)

Mix the ingredients together with enough flour and water so that the mixture stays together. Form into 8cm long croquets and fry until golden brown in hot oil.

Makes 12.

PAW PAW RAW BARLEY (Raw)

This is the perfect meal for the end of a perfect summer's day. (It is also a strange breakfast and a heavenly lunch...)

2 cups of pearled barley
1 cup of alfalfa sprouts
1 cup of chopped parsley
1/2 cup of chopped chives
2 cups of cottage cheese (or crumbled firm tofu)
2 ripe paw paws peeled and cubed
1/2 cup of lemon juice
1/4 cup of unrefined cold pressed sunflower seed oil
grated fresh coconut

Soak the barley in water for 24 hours then drain off the water. Mix ingredients together in a large salad bowl and sprinkle some fresh grated coconut over the top. Serve chilled.

We have also made this salad with rock melon and cantaloupe which is equally as delicious. The cottage cheese or tofu is not absolutely necessary to the success of the dish either.

Serves 4 large helpings or 6 side salads.

MEDITERRANEAN BARLEY

This pilaf is a good introduction to the delights of pearled barley for those who have only ever seen it at the bottom of a soup bowl. This is a version of a traditional recipe from northern Italy.

4 cups of cooked pearled barley (1 cup raw)
1 cup of chopped onion
2 chopped cloves of garlic
1/3 cup of olive oil
1 cubed medium eggplant
2 sliced courgettes
1 tsp of dried oregano
2 cups of sliced tomatoes
1/4 tsp of cayenne pepper

1 cup of grated mozzarella cheese

Sauté the onions and the garlic in the oil for 3 -5 minutes, adding the eggplant after 1 minute, then the courgettes. Cook for several minutes stirring frequently. Add the remaining ingredients except the cheese. Simmer until the vegetables are almost cooked.
Remove from heat, stir in the grated cheese, and serve.

Serves 6.

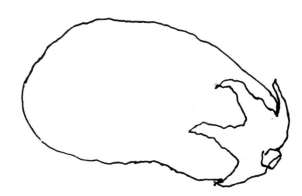

BARLEY FRITTERS
These are delicious little numbers, well worth a party or two.

1 cup of barley flour
1 cup of cooked pearled barley (1/4 cup raw)
1/4 cup of finely chopped spring onions
1/4 cup of finely chopped fresh parsley
1/2 cup of mashed avocado (or linseed binder - see page 10)
1/2 tsp of kelp powder
1/2 cup of water
olive oil

Mix the ingredients thoroughly into a thick batter. Drop by tablespoonfuls into a pan with the olive oil at a medium heat.
Fry for about 2 minutes each side, until lightly brown. Drain on absorbent paper and serve.

Makes about 8 fritters.

BARLEY BISCUITS

Yummy, yeasted biscuits. Our trials were so successful we made more and more. Substitute rice malt for the honey if you prefer a more balanced sweetener.

2 cups of barley flour
3/4 cup of warm water
1 tbsp of honey
2 tsps of active dried yeast
2 tbsp of butter (or unrefined sesame or sunflower oil)

Stir the yeast and honey into the warm water and leave for 15 minutes for the yeast to activate.

Cut the butter into the flour and rub it into pea-sized lumps. Add the yeast mixture and thoroughly blend all together. Leave for 5 minutes to rise.

Preheat the oven to 205°C (400°F). Drop spoonfuls of the dough onto an oiled baking tray and pat into 6cm rounds with the back of a wet spoon. Bake for 15-20 minutes until browned.

Makes about 12 biscuits.

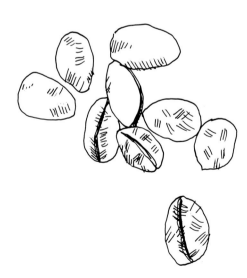

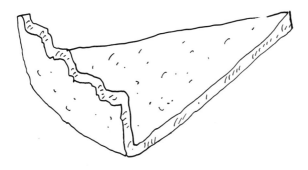

BARLEY-OAT PIECRUST
A light, incredibly edible short pastry.

1 cup of barley flour
1 cup of oat flour
1/3 cup of unrefined sunflower oil
about 1/2 cup of water

Mix the flours together in a bowl then add the oil. Work the oil evenly through the flour mixture. Add water gradually, mixing it in as you go, until a pliable dough is formed.

Press the dough into an oiled 22cm pie tin (or roll it out between two sheets of greaseproof paper). Prick evenly with a fork and bake at 205°C (400°F) for 10-15 minutes (this is a partly baked pie shell).

If you substitute oatmeal for the oat flour it makes a nice textured savoury piecrust although we found it tended to be a bit crumbly.

We made a delicious savoury pie filling using:

lightly sautéd chopped tomatoes
chopped fresh herbs
sliced red onion
mung bean sprouts
kernels of fresh sweet corn

You might like to try it. Partly bake the shell as above. Cook the filling in a pan then fill the pie shell and bake for another 15-20 minutes. Garnish with grated cheese and serve.

Makes plenty for 4.

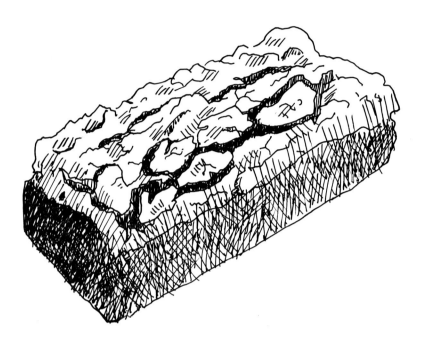

BARLEY-RICE BREAD

Barley flour gives a sweet cake-like quality if it is lightly pan-toasted before adding to the recipe.

      1 1/2 cups of barley flour
      1 1/2 cups of brown rice flour
      1 1/2 cups of water
      2 tbsps of baking powder (see alternative on page11)
      1/4 cup of unrefined sesame oil

First mix the flours and the baking powder together. Stir in the oil and water and mix into a sticky dough.

Put the dough in an oiled bread tin and bake at 175° C (350°F) for 60 minutes. Remove from oven and cover until cool to retain moisture.

Makes 1 loaf.

CORN

Description

Corn, yellow corn or maize as it is otherwise known, is a tall sturdy member of the family of grasses, with varieties growing to heights of up to three metres. The grains form in a cob which develops in the axil of the leaf midway up the stem of the plant. Cobs are generally left on the plants to fully mature and dry before harvesting. Corn is a close relation of sweetcorn, which is eaten as a fresh vegetable. However the sugars in maize corn are fully converted to starches, which enables it to be milled into flour, and it has a higher proportion of protein.

History

Although the date of the origin of domesticated maize is still being debated by archaeologists it seems it originated about 3500 BC in South and Central America. The civilisations of the Incas, the Mayans and the Aztec were all dependant on cultivated corn as their major food source. It also became a staple food of the American Indian cultures and spread throughout North America. The North American Indians used the corn plant as a focus for many religious ceremonies. The plant was known as *Daughter of Life* and *Seed of seeds*.

Today corn is still grown and prepared traditionally in these areas but it has also been a traditional food for centuries in parts of Africa and Europe. Whereas flatbreads were the tradition in the Latin countries, in Africa and Europe the corn was usually ground and boiled into a porridge.

In northern Italy boiled cornmeal, *polenta*, is a traditional dish. Polenta is often cooled and fried in oil as a substitute for wheatbread.

Hominy grits are a traditional cornmeal dish from the southern United States. Corn kernels are soaked in lye which removes the indigestible skin. The kernels are then washed, boiled and dried. At this stage they are milled into a coarse meal known as hominy grits and used in breads, stews and porridges.

Uses and Preparation

Corn is very high in natural oils. Large mills usually remove the oils by toasting the grain so that rancidity cannot occur. This corn is sold as de-germed corn. Unfortunately this removes one of the main benefits corn has as a food. Some smaller mills are now making available full-germ corn meals and flours which are 100 % wholegrain. These products are more flavoursome and better nutritionally provided they can be bought fresh.

Whole corn is delicious sprouted and can be used as the basis for salads, soups and baked foods. However corn is more widely used as a milled grain, either as coarse or fine cornmeal, or maize cornflour. Extra fine real maize cornflour is superb for light cakes, sponges and thickening. The bright yellow colour of the grain and the textures of the cornmeals and flours add extra delight to different dishes.

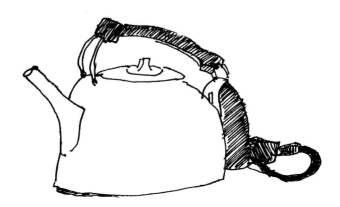

CORN SPROUT MUESLI (Raw)
An unusual muesli with a rich corn flavour.

>1 cup of minced corn sprouts (maize or sweetcorn seed)
>1/4 cup of sunflower seeds
>1/4 cup of pumpkin seeds
>1/4 cup of raisins
>1/4 cup of chopped almonds
>1/4 cup of shredded coconut
>1 1/2 cups of chopped fresh fruit

Mix the ingredients together and serve in bowls with yogurt, milk, soymilk, fruit juice or water.

Do not use seed treated for sowing. To be sure of uncontaminated seed dry some cobs from your own harvest for use throughout the year.

Serves 2.

FINEST CORNMEAL PORRIDGE
Good texture for babies.

>1/2 cup of fine cornmeal
>1/2 cup of cold water
>1/2 cup of chopped fresh fruit or soaked dried fruit
>2 cups of boiling water

Stir cold water into the cornmeal in a saucepan. Add boiling water and cook on a medium heat for 10-15 minutes until the porridge is thick. Mix in the fruit and serve.

Serves 2.

CORNMEAL PIE SHELLS
Crunchy, crumbly scrummy pie shells.

1 cup of maize cornflour
1/2 cup of fine cornmeal
1/4 cup of unrefined sunflower oil (or butter)
about 1/2 cup of water

Preheat the oven to 220° C (425°F). Mix the cornflour and cornmeal together in a bowl. Either mix the oil into the flour thoroughly, or if using butter cut it into the mixture in small lumps and rub it into the flour until it looks like even crumbs.

Sprinkle the water on gradually, stirring it in thoroughly with a fork. Add only enough water so the mixture forms a cohesive soft dough. Press the dough straight into the oiled piedish or roll the dough out on a floured surface into a circle just larger than the piedish. Transfer the rolled dough to the piedish by wrapping it around the rolling pin. The dough tends to break easily and can be patched up in the piedish by pressing broken edges together or pressing in scraps to cover holes. Trim the edges and press into the piedish.

At this stage the shell can be fully baked, partly baked or filled unbaked. To partly bake, prick shell all over evenly with a fork, fill with one layer of dried beans to keep the shell flat and bake for 10 minutes.

For a fully baked shell remove the beans after 10 minutes and bake for another 10 minutes until the crust is crisp and lightly browned.

Use the same recipe to make a pie crust top for the pie.

Makes one 22cm pie crust.

GREEN TOMATO CORNCRUST PIE
A rare delight.

1 cornmeal pie shell (partly baked)
1 cornmeal pie crust top (optional)
1/2 cup of honey or rice malt
1/3 cup of maize cornflour
1/4 tsp salt (optional)
1/2 tsp of mixed spice
1/2 cup of chopped red pepper
8 green tomatoes
1/2 cup of raisins
1/3 cup of vinegar (tarragon, or mint vinegar is very nice)

Mix honey, flour, salt, spice, raisins, red pepper and vinegar in a bowl. Slice the tomatoes and toss them in this mixture.

Lay the slices in a partly-baked pie shell and sprinkle the remaining mixture over them. Place the top uncooked pie crust on the pie, if you want a top crust; crimp the edges and prick the crust liberally with a fork to let steam escape.

Bake at 195°C (380°F) for 30 minutes until the crust browns slightly.

Serves 4-6 with a 22cm pie.

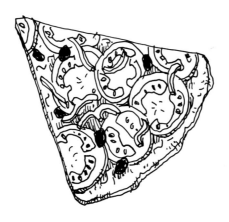

POLENTA
A rustic dish from the north of Italy.

1 cup of medium cornmeal
4 cups of water
1 cup of grated parmesan or romano cheese (optional)

Mix the water and cornmeal in a large saucepan and bring to the boil stirring constantly. Simmer on a low heat for about 20 minutes until cooked. Add half the cheese, mix in well then turn into an oiled casserole. Sprinkle remaining cheese on top and bake at 180°C (350°F) for 15 minutes or until lightly brown on top.

Serve with a spicy tomato sauce. For variation try adding a teaspoon of dried basil and some chopped onion.

Serves 5.

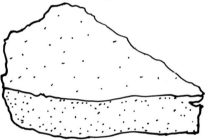

TORTILLAS
Fresh tortillas are an uncommon treat. Be prepared, it takes some practice to shape perfect, round, thin tortillas at the first slap of the dough. Our first ones were a bit thick but they tasted great.

1 cup of boiling water
1 cup of fine cornmeal
1 tsp of salt (optional)

Pour the boiling water over the cornmeal (and salt), stirring until thick. Pat into thin cakes 15cm in diameter when the mixture is cool enough. If you are having difficulty making the cakes thin enough try rolling out the dough between two sheets of greaseproof paper.These cakes can either be browned both sides on an un-greased griddle or pan, or deep fried.

Suitably fine cornmeals are sometimes hard to find, if this is so try adding some maize cornflour to your fine cornmeal to make a better dough.

Stack your tortillas between sheets of greaseproof paper while you are preparing them. They are then easy to peel off to cook.

Makes 6 tortillas.

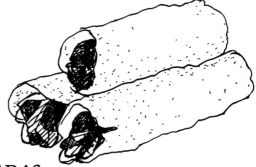

SPINACH ENCHILADAS

12 fresh corn tortillas (double above recipe)
500g of fresh washed spinach
1 chopped onion
2 finely chopped cloves of garlic
300g of grated cheese (optional)
1/4 tsp salt (optional)
unrefined olive oil

Sauté the garlic and the onion in a little oil for 1-2 minutes. Chop the spinach and add it to the pan cooking it at a medium heat for another 5 minutes (with the salt).

Brush a fresh tortilla with some oil and heat it both sides in a pan until it is soft. Spread a tablespoon of grated cheese down the centre with another tablespoon of the spinach mixture over the top of the cheese.

Fold one end of the tortilla over the filling and roll it up. Continue until either the tortillas or the mixture is used up.

Place the enchiladas in an oiled casserole and bake at 175°C (350°F) for 15-20 minutes.

Serve with a hot, spicy sauce.

Makes 12.

CORNMEAL PATTIES

2 cups of cornmeal
1/2 cup of chopped nuts
1/4 cup of sesame seeds
1/4 cup of chopped parsley
unsalted food yeast

Cook the cornmeal with about 8 cups of water, into a mush, and cool. Mix in the other ingredients, adding enough unsalted food yeast to season. Form into patties about 6cm in diameter. Place on a greased tray and bake at 180°C (350°F) for 30 minutes.

Serve either hot or cold with a sauce or relish.

Makes 8.

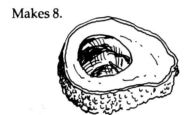

AVOCADO CORN MUFFINS

For a savoury or sweet cake these little fellas provide some melting moments.

2 cups of fine cornmeal
1 cup of mashed avocado
1 tsp of baking powder (see alternative on page 11)
1/2 cup of soymilk (or milk)
1/4 cup of unrefined sunflower oil
1/4 cup of honey or rice malt (optional)

Mix the cornmeal and the baking powder together. Add the remaining ingredients and beat into a thick batter.

Spoon the mixture into an oiled muffin tray. Bake for 20-30 minutes at 205°C (400°F).

Makes 12.

PEANUT BUTTER PUDDING
A crunchy custard.

> 1/2 cup of maize cornflour
> 1/2 cup of honey (or rice malt)
> 1 cup of crunchy peanut butter
> 1/2 tsp of pure vanilla essence
> 4 cups of fresh soymilk (or milk)

Put the maize cornflour into a saucepan and gradually stir in the soymilk. When the mixture is smooth and thickening place on a low heat and mix in the honey, stirring constantly.

Bring to the boil, then simmer for 2-3 minutes. Remove from heat and stir in the peanut butter and vanilla essence.

Serve with fresh chopped fruit, yogurt or cream.

Serves 4.

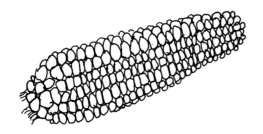

SPICY MAIZE APPLECAKE
Moist and unusual.

1 cup of maize cornflour
1/2 cup of arrowroot powder (or soy flour)
1 1/2 cups of grated apple
1 cup of muscatel raisins
1 tsp ground cloves
1 tsp ground nutmeg
3/4 cup of apple juice (or water)
2 tsp of baking powder (see alternative on page 11)
1/4 cup of unrefined sunflower oil

Mix the maize cornflour with the arrowroot, raisins, spices and baking powder, then beat in the remaining ingredients to form a thick batter. Pour this mixture into an oiled cake tin.

Bake for about 60 minutes at 175°C (350°F). Remove from the oven and cover while cooling.

Makes 1 cake.

SIOUX PUDDING
Sweet and rich.

  2/3 cup of cornmeal
  3 cups of milk (or soymilk)
  1/4 cup of unrefined corn oil or butter
  1/4 cup of maple syrup (or honey, or rice malt)
  1 tbsp of molasses
  1 tsp of cinnamon
  1/2 tsp of ground nutmeg

Heat 2 1/2 cups of the milk with the spices and stir in the butter, maple syrup and molasses. Slowly mix the cornmeal into this, stirring constantly. Cook at a low temperature for about 10 minutes until thick. Stir frequently to avoid the mixture sticking.

Pour into a casserole, tip on 1/2 cup of milk and bake at 150°C (300°F) for 1 1/2 hours.

Serves 6.

CORNBREAD

This is a version of a traditional recipe from southern United States.

> 2 cups of fine cornmeal
> 1/2 cup coarse cornmeal
> 1/2 cup of soy flour
> 1 tsp baking powder (see alternative on page 11)
> 1 tbsp unrefined corn oil
> 2 cups of milk or soymilk
> 1/2 tsp salt (optional)

Mix dry ingredients then add the oil and milk. Turn into a well greased bread tin and bake at 190°C (375°F) for 40-50 minutes.

This recipe is lifted to even greater heights with the addition of 1/2 cup of minced sweetcorn kernels and 2 finely chopped cloves of garlic.

Makes 1 loaf.

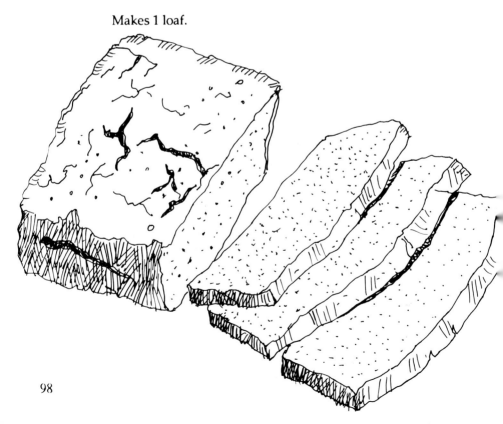

OATS

Description

Oats are a cereal grain from the same family of grasses that includes wheat, maize, rice and millet. They thrive in cool temperate climates and the grain ripens even in short wet summers. Strong germination and vigour have been retained from the wild oat ancestors which were regarded as a nuisance weed by farmers as they would become established in other domestic crops.

The seed does not form in a bunched head like wheat, barley and rye, but hangs from the stem in individual grains. The grain separates easily from the hulls with a light threshing.

Several cultivars are commercially grown today. Not only are they each suited to different conditions but each also has a different appearance. Jumbo oats are from a cultivar that produces large fat golden oats. Other cultivars produce different sized grain with a range of colour from grey to golden yellow.

History

The earliest samples of the common domesticated oat have been found in caves in Switzerland, dating back to 2000 BC. It seems these oats were domesticated from the wild oats native to northwest Europe.

Although cultivated oats date back to about 400 BC in Britain it is not until the Middle Ages that evidence is available showing oats were a popular part of the basic diet. In Scotland and northern England oatmeal porridge and oatbread were traditional foods. *Dredgecorn*, a mixture of oats and barley, was also frequently used as a foundation for stews.

In Wales oatmeal broth and oatcakes are still traditional dishes and in the north of France oatmeal has the longstanding local name of *Breton gruel*.

With industrialisation oats fell from favour, being regarded as peasant food or stock food by the upwardly mobile industrialising countries. However, in the last 50 years, oats have regained their popularity and today rolled oats and oatmeal form a large part of our cereal diet.

Uses and Preparation

Oats are a rich foodstore. Not only have they more protein than wheat or rice but they have more vitamin B1 (thiamine) than any other cereal grain.

They are also rich in the other B vitamins, oil, iron and phosphorus. There are trace elements of copper, manganese, zinc and potassium. Oats form a balanced protein diet when eaten with dairy products.

Although the grain is the most popular food from the plant, the fresh green leaves are superb for juicing and the dried hulls and oatstraw make a delicious calcium rich tea.

The unhulled oat is not readily digestible, however both hulled and unhulled oats are suitable for sprouting. They only require a short soaking (about 6 hours) and are at their best when the sprout is about the same length as the grain itself. Oat sprouts are sweet tasting and high in B vitamins; they can be used in place of wheat sprouts in most recipes.

Hulled oats are usually processed into rolled oats, oatmeal or oat flour, although oat bran has become a fashionable food recently due to discoveries associating it with the reduction of cholesterol. Rather than create another extracted miracle product we feel our health is best served by eating a balanced wholefood diet in which one would receive the benefits of the oat bran by eating flours and cereals made with whole oats.

Once oats are milled or rolled the oil is exposed and oxidises on contact with the air. This is rancidity and can be tasted as a bitterness in stale flours and oatmeals. Because of the high oil content most rolled oats, oatmeals and flours are heated in the milling and rolling process to eliminate the oils (and consequently much of the nutritional value). Uncooked rolled oats, oatmeals and flours are available from some health food specialists and are much more nutritious but must be bought freshmilled or vacuum sealed.

Stoneground oat flour is a soft flour with a fine texture and delicious flavour. It browns well and is excellent for sauces and thickening. Oat flour is very suitable for biscuits and pancakes and can be used in place of wheat flour. For cakes however a 50/50 mix with wheat flour maintains the same lightness and texture.

OAT SUNRISE (Raw)

    1 cup of sprouted oats
    1/2 cup of chopped sunflower seeds
    1/2 cup of raisins
    1 sliced banana
    2 peeled sliced oranges
    1/2 cup of mashed soft tofu

Mix the ingredients lightly together and serve.

Breakfast for 2.

IRONSIDES OATMEAL BREAKFAST

Dave played guitar like a-ringin a bell, he was also a mobile man and lived on the wing. When he touched down long enough for food this was his regular breakfast. He said it was a 'brick in the stomach' and lasted him all day.

    1/2 cup of rolled oats
    1/2 cup of oatmeal
    1/2 cup of raisins
    1/2 cup of chopped nuts or seeds
    1/2 tsp of cinnamon
    2 cups of cold water

Mix it all together in a saucepan and bring to the boil. Reduce heat and cook for 10 minutes. Pour into bowls and serve with honey, milk, soymilk or yogurt.

Serves 2 (or one if you're hungry).

PAPRIKA-SUNFLOWER PÂTÉ (Raw)
Never has raw food tasted so exquisite, so sophisticated...

1 cup of rolled oats
1 cup of sunflower seeds
1 cup of finely grated carrot
1/2 cup of finely chopped onion
1 tsp of sage
1 tsp of thyme
1 tsp of dry mustard
1 tsp of unrefined sunflower oil
1/2 cup of water

Mince, grind or chop the sunflower seeds finely. Mix in a bowl with the other dry ingredients. Gradually add the water until the mixture is just wet enough to hold together.

Press into a lightly oiled bread loaf tin and chill for 1 hour. Turn out upside down on a plate, sprinkle with paprika and garnish with parsley and slices of orange.

Serves 4.

LEMON-OATMEAL SOUP
Lemon and oatmeal seem to have a natural affinity for each other. This combination is hearty and satisfying yet light on the palate.

1/2 cup of oatmeal
1 chopped onion
2 finely chopped cloves of garlic
1 cup of chopped mixed vegetables
1 tsp of soy sauce
1/2 tsp of fresh or dried chopped sage
2 tsps of unsalted food yeast
5 cups of water or vegetable stock
1 halved lemon
chopped parsley
cooking oil

Sauté the onion, garlic and oatmeal in a small amount of oil for 2-3 minutes. Combine all the ingredients in a soup pot and simmer for 25-30 minutes.

Take out the 2 lemon halves and discard them, pour the soup into bowls and serve with a garnish of chopped parsley.

Serves 6.

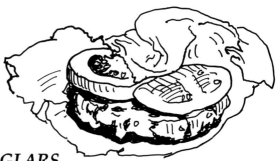

OAT-SOY BURGLARS

An Indian visitor loved having ' burglars' for dinner. These rich, tasty vegetarian burgers are dedicated to her.

1 cup of cooked oatmeal
1 cup of cooked, mashed soybeans
1/4 cup of ground or finely chopped sunflower seeds
1/2 cup of grated raw potato
1/2 cup of chopped onion
1/2 cup of grated carrot
1/2 tsp of fresh chopped thyme
1/3 cup of fresh chopped parsley
1/2 cup of fresh chopped sage
1/2 cup of breadcrumbs or wheatgerm
water
cooking oil
flour

Mix all the ingredients together thoroughly. Add water if necessary, so the mixture can be formed into patties. Dust these with flour and fry in a little oil on a medium heat for about 3 minutes on each side until brown

Makes 10.

FRUITY FREEZE (Raw)

1 cup of rolled oats
1 tbsp wheatgerm
1/2 cup of mixed nuts
1 1/2 cups of chopped fresh fruit
1 mashed banana
1/3 cup of raisins
2 tbsp fruit juice or water
1 tsp cinnamon
1/4 tsp of natural almond essence (take care this essence is
strong)

Grind or chop the nuts and then mash the fruit together. Mix the remaining ingredients into this mixture until it is just moist. Add more oats if necessary.

Spoon the mixture into a small loaf tin and freeze for about 2 hours. Turn out onto a plate, leave for a few minutes, and serve in slices.

Serves 4.

OATMEAL PIE DOUGH

*My mother gave her unqualified seal of approval to the recipe for
this pie shell and the following banana filling. She even had more.*

1 cup of fresh oat flour
1/2 cup of oatmeal
1/3 cup of unrefined sunflower oil (or butter)
about 1/4 cup of water

Mix the oat flour and oatmeal in a bowl. Rub in the oil (or
butter) until the mixture crumbs evenly. Sprinkle the water on a
little at a time and mix it in well until the mixture forms a dough.

Press the dough out by hand on a floured board and then roll
it (with plenty of dusting with oat flour) to about 5mm thick. Fit the
dough into the piedish, patching any holes where necessary.

Prick the bottom all over with a fork and bake at 220° C
(425°F) for 10 minutes. This will give you a partly baked shell. Bake
for another 8-10 minutes until the shell starts to brown for a fully
baked pie shell.

This coarse textured pie shell is perfect for sweet, smooth
dessert fillings such as the one following. Use the same quantities
as above to make a pie crust.

Makes one 22cm pie shell.

BAHAMA BANANA FOR BALARAMA (Raw)

A delicious dessert deserving of royalty. It is guaranteed to drop your eyelids several centimetres (you may even swoon).

> 1 fully baked oatmeal pie shell
> 300g of soft tofu
> 3 sliced bananas
> 2 tbsps of honey
> 2 tbsps of melted butter (optional)
> 1/2 tsp cinnamon
> 1/4 tsp of pure vanilla essence
> grated rind of one lemon
> cinnamon for topping

Blend the tofu with the honey, spice and vanilla essence. Lightly fold in the sliced bananas, lemon rind (and butter).

Pour this mixture into the pie shell. Sprinkle cinnamon over the top. Chill and serve.

Makes one 22cm pie.

APPLE-OAT CRUMBLE

A tasty alternative to the traditional wheat flour crumble.

> 1 cup of oatmeal
> 1/2 cup of rolled oats
> 1/2 cup of brown rice flour
> 3 cups of cored and sliced apples
> 1/3 cup of unrefined sunflower oil (or butter)
> 2 tbsps of honey
> 1/4 tsp of mixed spice
> juice from one lemon

Mix the apples, lemon juice, and spice and place in a casserole. Melt the butter, or mix the oil, with the honey for the crumble and combine it with the oatmeal, rolled oats and brown rice flour.

Sprinkle this over the apples and bake at 175°C (350°F) for 30 minutes.

Makes enough for 5-6.

BLISS BALLS (Raw)
A rich after dinner sweet - one ball goes a long way. They are lovely.

1 cup of mixed nuts (almonds, brazils, peanuts)
1 cup of rolled oats
1 cup of stoned dates
1 tbsp of tahini (ground sesame seed butter)
1 tbsp water
rice flour or fine shredded coconut

Mince the ingredients finely. Form into balls about 3cm in diameter and roll in rice flour or fine shredded coconut. Keep in the refrigerator.

Makes about 10.

DATE OATIES
Quick and easy to make.

1 cup of rolled oats
1/2 cup of oatmeal
1/2 cup of rice flour
1/2 cup of chopped dates
120g of butter
1 tbsp of honey
1 mashed banana
1/4 tsp of pure vanilla essence
1/4 cup of water

Mix the butter, honey, banana, vanilla essence and water together. Stir in the remaining ingredients and mix well.

Drop the mixture by dessertspoonfuls on to an oiled baking tray. Bake at 175°C (350°F) for 15-20 minutes until biscuits brown on top.

Makes 12.

OAT WAFERS
A simple, delightful biscuit from the north of England.

1 cup of oat flour
1 tbsp butter or unrefined sunflower oil
1/4 cup of warm water
pinch of salt (optional)

Mix the ingredients thoroughly into a soft dough. Roll out on a floured board as thin as possible. Cut out with shaped cutters or into squares by hand and sprinkle with oat flour.

Cook the wafers on a hot griddle or heavy bottomed pan for about 4 minutes. Grill the top brown and crisp. These biscuits are traditionally served with jam and whipped cream.

Makes about 12.

PEANUT COCONUT BISCUITS

3 cups of oat flour
1 cup of minced or chopped peanuts
1/2 cup of fresh grated coconut or desiccated fine coconut
2 tbsps of honey
1/4 cup of oil
1 cup of water

Mix the ingredients together, adding the water last, to form a stiff dough. Form into balls about 4cm in diameter and place them on a floured baking tray. Press the balls down with a wet fork into flat biscuits.
Bake at 175°C (350°F) for 30 minutes until lightly browned. Remove from the oven and transfer to a wire rack to cool.

Makes 20 biscuits.

OAT CRUNCH

Not a very healthy biscuit but delicious. Try adding chopped nuts or sunflower seeds.

2 cups of rolled oats
1 cup of desiccated coconut
1/2 cup of honey
120g of butter

Melt the butter and honey together. Mix in the other ingredients and press into an oiled cake tin.
Bake at 190°C (375°F) for 15-20 minutes until brown. Remove from the oven and slice while still hot - but leave in the biscuit tray until cool!

Makes 12 pieces.

OAT-RYE BREAD

1 cup of rolled oats
1 1/2 cups of extra-fine wholemeal flour
1 1/2 cups of wholemeal flour
1/2 cup of soy flour
1 cup of rye flour
1 1/4 cups of warm water
1/2 tbsp active dried yeast
2 tsps honey
2 tbsps caraway seeds
1/2 tsp salt (optional)
1 tbsp of unrefined sunflower oil

Dissolve the yeast in the warm water with the honey. Add 1 cup of wholemeal flour and beat for 5 minutes until the mixture is a batter. Leave this to rise in a warm place for 15 minutes then slowly add the remaining flour, mixing well before adding the next cupful.

As soon as the dough stays in one piece tip it onto a floured board and knead it for at least 10 minutes. When it is well kneaded form it into a ball, brush the surface with oil, cover, and leave in a bowl to rise for 60 minutes. Press the dough down and leave to rise for a further 45 minutes. Shape the dough into a loaf and roll it in 1 1/2 tbsps of caraway seeds. Place this in an oiled bread tin and leave to rise for 20-30 minutes in a warm place.

Sprinkle the left-over caraway seeds on top of the loaf and bake at 175° C (350° F) for 50-60 minutes. Remove from the oven, de-tin and cool on a wire rack.

Makes 1 loaf.

PEAS

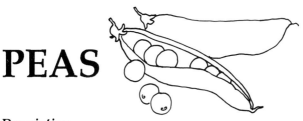

Description

Peas are the seeds of an annual vine produced in pods. Field peas, used for milling or dried whole, are members of the large family *Pisum*. This family also includes garden peas and sugar peas.

Many varieties of field peas are grown commercially today. The three main categories are blue peas, maple peas and white peas. The varieties differ markedly in their size, colour, flavour and growing conditions.

We have preferred organically grown blue peas for milling, sprouting and cooking whole. The blue colour gives a deep green flour which makes attractive soups and baked goods. Their flavour is superb and they germinate very well. Yellow peas and marrowfat peas both mill into good flour and are suitable for the following recipes also.

History

Although the cultivation of lentils and field beans has been traced back to about 6500 BC, the domestication of field peas is more obscure. It seems the plant originated in the area between the Tigris and Euphrates rivers in North Africa. Peas have been found in relics from Stone Age cultures. Both the Ancient Greek and Roman cultures harvested peas as a food crop but it was only when the cultivation of peas spread into the colder climates of northern Europe that they became a significant part of man's diet.

By the Middle Ages field peas had become an important crop throughout Europe and Britain where they were harvested and dried for use as a winter food (the early English pease pudding dates from these times).

It was not until the seventeenth century that peas became popular as a fresh vegetable. Fresh green peas became a fad at the court of Louis XIV in France; the French aristocracy would rush home from the theatre to eat platefuls of young green peas. The rapid growth in popularity of peas-in-the-pod was advanced by early commercial plant breeders who produced hybrid varietes of garden peas, suitable for eating fresh, from the mid eighteenth century.

From this time the popularity of dried peas has declined in the West. However varieties of dried peas and pea flours are still an important food source in India and throughout Asia.

Uses and Preparation

Sprouted blue peas are a delicious addition to any salad or stew. Peas sprout quickly and germinate well. They have a flavour similar to fresh peas and are much sweeter than if simply soaked and cooked. Sprouted peas have about 20% protein and are high in vitamins A,B and C. They also have good proportions of phosphorus and potassium.

As well as being a flavoursome addition to any savoury dish using flour, pea flour has a special value as a binder for diets avoiding wheat, eggs or dairy products.

The flavour of blue pea flour is characteristic and strong for a flour and is best reserved for savoury dishes. Yellow pea flour has a milder flavour and is more versatile. Pea flours are useful in soups and stews for thickening and adding flavour.

Baking with pea flour is very rewarding. It is good to blend pea flour 50/50 with wheat flour recipes for breads, flatbreads, pancakes and savoury crackers or as a blend with any bland tasting flours.

PEA STUFFED MUSHROOMS (Raw)

1/2 cup of chopped sprouted blue peas
8 large button mushrooms
75g of soft tofu (or cottage cheese)
1 chopped tomato
1/2 tbsp chopped fresh mint
1/2 tbsp chopped fresh parsley
1/2 tbsp chopped fresh basil
juice of one lemon
wedges of lemon

Wash the mushrooms remove the stalks and place them to one side. Mash the tofu and mix it with the other ingredients. Spoon an equal portion of this filling into each mushroom making a mound.

Sprinkle with paprika and serve on a bed of lettuce with wedges of lemon.

Serves 4.

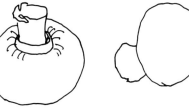

TAHINI PEA DIP (Raw)

A dip wih a lovely texture and that I-must-have-another-one quality. Try it with Basic Buckwheat Biscuits (on page 63).

2 cups of sprouted peas
1/2 cup of tahini (ground sesame seed butter)
juice of one lemon
2 tsps of soy sauce
2 finely chopped cloves of garlic
1/2 cup of chopped mint
1/4 tsp of chilli powder

Blend the ingredients together to make a firm dip. Serve chilled with raw carrot and celery fingers or savoury crackers.

PEASE PUDDING

The word pea *came from the Old English* pease *which was borrowed from the Latin* pisum *which was borrowed from the Sanscrit* pis *meaning piece of pod. This is a traditional English dish dating back to early medieval times.*

2 cups of blue peas, or split green peas (soaked for 12hrs)
1 tbsp butter or unrefined sunflower oil
herbs
unsalted food yeast (optional)
salt, pepper (optional)

Bring the peas to the boil then simmer for 30 minutes. Drain and purée or mash the peas thoroughly with the butter (or oil) and seasonings. Tip the mixture on to a muslin cloth and tie into a ball leaving a length of string loose. Simmer the muslin ball in water for 1 hour. Turn the pudding out onto a dish and serve.

Chopped onions and herbs can be added to the stock water to give more flavour.

Although traditionally pease pudding was often an accompaniment to bacon or ham, it is also a great dish to have with ratatouille and salads.

PEASE PUDDING BAKED

The mashed mixture of seasoned peas, with the addition of 1/2 cup of the cooking water, can also be placed into an oiled loaf tin and baked as a vegetable loaf.

Bake at 190°C (375°F) for 30-40 minutes.

This dish is enhanced with a good, rich sauce. We used this oat flour herb sauce:

Sauté 1/2 chopped onion in a little oil and add 2 tbsps of oat flour. Slowly stir in 2 cups of water or stock and add 1/2 tsp of thyme.

Serves 6.

BLUE PEA TERRINE
Served on a bed of lettuce with some slices of tomato and cucumber this terrine is a lovely meal for a hot summer's night.

2 cups of blue peas (soaked for 12hrs)
1 cup of finely chopped fresh parsley
4 cloves of finely chopped garlic
1/2 tsp sage
1/2 tsp thyme
2 tsps curry powder
2 tsps caraway seed
1/2 cup of unsalted food yeast
2 tsps of agar agar

Cook the peas for 30 minutes until soft then mash. Apart from the agar agar mix in the other ingredients. While still hot, sprinkle the agar agar into the mixture little by little and mix in well. (*Agar agar* is an extract from a sea vegetable which forms a jelly similar to gelatine, most healthfood stores stock it.)

Spoon the mixture into an oiled dish and chill for 1 - 2 hours. Turn the terrine onto a plate, garnish with mint and slices of lemon, and serve.

Serves 4-6.

INSTANT PEA SOUP

1 cup of blue pea flour
1 chopped onion
3 minced cloves of garlic
5 cups of vegetable stock or water
1/2 cup of chopped mint
1 cup of sour cream (optional)
1 tbsp of oil

In a soup pot sauté the onion and garlic in the oil for 2 minutes. Add the flour and cook a further 2 minutes. Slowly add the water, stirring all the time. Simmer for 5 minutes stirring frequently.

Remove from heat and stir in the chopped mint (and sour cream). Serve with freshly baked bread.

Serves 4.

PEAFLOUR PAKORAS

Not a very healthy recipe in itself but serve them with salads and raita and a new dimension arises.

1 cup of pea flour
2 cups of chopped vegetables (carrots, onions, broccoli etc)
3/4 tsp of garam marsala
1/2 tsp of chilli powder
1/4 tsp of turmeric
3/4 cup of water

1/2 tsp salt (optional)
oil for deep frying

Beat the flour into the water to form a batter. Add the spices, vegetables (and salt) and mix well.

Heat the oil and drop dessertspoonfuls of the mixture gently into the oil and fry until golden brown. Drain on absorbent paper and serve with tomato chutney (see page 23) and chopped mint.

Serves 4-6.

SPROUTED PEALAF
An easy dish to make with an unusual , slightly oriental flavour.

1 cup of sprouted blue peas
1 chopped onion
1 tsp of whole cumin seeds
1 1/2 cups of long grain brown rice
2 tbsps unsalted food yeast
2 cups of water
1/2 cup of chopped parsley
soy sauce
cooking oil

Sauté the onion and the cumin seeds in a small amount of oil for 2-3 minutes. Add the rice, blue peas, food yeast and water, stir well. Bring to the boil then cover and simmer on a low heat for 20 minutes until the rice is cooked. Check from time to time, extra water may need to be added.

Stir in the chopped parsley and season with soy sauce to taste. Genuine *tamari* soy sauce is wheat free with a richer, less salty flavour.

Serves 4-6.

BOMBAY SPROUTED PEA
Surprisingly this is very mild but what flavour!

2 cups of sprouted blue peas
2 chopped onions
1 small piece of fresh ginger (about 2cm) chopped
3 medium potatoes, scrubbed and cubed
3 quartered tomatoes
1 tsp whole cumin seeds
1/2 tsp of ground cardamom
1/4 tsp of ground cloves
1 tbsp of ground cumin
1 tbsp of ground coriander
1 tsp of curry powder
1 cup of plain unsweetened yogurt
1/4 cup of cooking oil
1/2 cup of water

Sauté the onions, ginger, spices and curry powder in the oil for 2-3 minutes. Reduce the heat and add the potatoes, yogurt and water. Cook for 15 minutes stirring frequently. Add the sprouted peas and tomatoes and cook for another 15 minutes.

Serve on a bed of boiled rice with lemon pickle and cucumber raita (see next recipe).

Serves 4.

CUCUMBER RAITA
This is a traditional accompaniment to many Indian dishes. It provides a light clean flavour to the palate and a fresh texture to contrast with the traditional curries and fried foods.

1 cucumber
1 chopped onion
2 cups of yogurt

1/2 tsp of ground cumin
pinch of cayenne
salt (optional)

Peel and de-seed the cucumber. Chop it finely and mix wih the other ingredients. Banana can be substituted for cucumber.
Serve chilled with curries and other savoury Indian dishes.

Makes enough for 4.

INDIAN PEA STEW

This is a great winter meal, brought to perfection when served with freshly baked chapatis (see page 26) and cucumber raita. It is mild yet flavoursome.

2 cups of blue peas (soaked for 12hrs)
1 chopped onion
1 tsp turmeric
2 1/2 cups of water
1 tsp of mango powder (optional)
1 tsp whole cumin seeds
1/2 tsp of chilli powder
1/2 cup of cooking oil (or ghee or butter)
paprika
chopped parsley

Sauté the onion for 2-3 minutes then add the blue peas and turmeric. After cooking for a further 2-3 minutes add the water and simmer for 25 minutes.
Add the mango powder, whole cumin seeds and chilli powder. Stir well and cook for another 10 minutes.
Serve in soup bowls. Garnish with chopped parsley, a sprinkle of paprika and a dob of yogurt.

Serves 4-6.

PEASPROUT SUNBREAD

2 cups of sprouted peas
2 cups of sprouted wheat or rye
1 tsp of ground cumin

Mince all the sprouts together finely (put them through twice if necessary). Mix in the ground cumin, knead for 5 minutes and form into a round loaf.

Place this on an oiled baking tray and bake at 135°C (280°F) for 2 hours.

Makes 1 loaf.

COOKING TIMES FOR GRAINS

(Soaking the grain for 12 hours first, reduces the cooking time by half.)

Grain	Uncooked Cups	Water	Boiling time	Cooked Cups
Barley	1	4	30-40 minutes	4
Buckwheat	1	3	20 minutes	3
Cornmeal	1	4	30 minutes	4
Millet	1	4	25 minutes	3
Oatmeal	1	2	10 minutes	3 1/2
Peas	1	4	60 minutes	4
Rice Brown	1	3	35 minutes	2 1/2
Rye	1	4	50 minutes	3
Triticale	1	4	50 minutes	2 1/2
Wheat	1	4	50 minutes	2 1/2

MEASURE CONVERSION

We have used the following conventions:
tsp   = teaspoon
tbsp   = tablespoon

All measurements are level and in metric standard cups, tea-spoons and tablespoons. American cups are only 200mls, about three quarters the size of the metric standard. The British imperial and metric standard sizes seem to be the same.

1 teaspoon   = 5 mls
1 tablespoon   = 15 mls
1 cup   = 250 mls

INDEX OF RECIPES
With easy reference chart for allergens.
(All recipes are egg-free, sugar-free, and low salt if any)

Recipe	Page	Wheat Free	Gluten Free	Dairy Free	Yeast Free	Raw
Almond Fried Rice	30	✓	✓	✓	✓	
Almond-Millet Tofu Log	67	✓	✓	✓	✓	✓
Almond Toes	36	✓	✓	✓	✓	
Apple-Oat Crumble	106	✓		✓	✓	
Arabian Spinach Pies	24			✓		
Avocado Barley Pancakes	78	✓		✓		
Avocado Corn Muffins	94	✓	✓	✓	✓	
Bahama Banana for Balarama	106	✓		✓	✓	
Banana Barley Pancakes	77	✓		✓	✓	
Banana Rice Biscuits	35	✓	✓	✓	✓	
Barley Biscuits	84	✓		✓		
Barley Broth	80	✓		✓	✓	
Barley-Buckwheat Pancakes	78	✓		✓		
Barley Fritters	83	✓		✓	✓	
Barley-Oat Piecrust	85	✓		✓	✓	
Barley Rice Bread	86	✓		✓	✓	
Barley Rissoles	81	✓		✓	✓	
Basic Buckwheat Biscuits	63	✓	✓	✓	✓	
Bliss Balls	107	✓		✓	✓	✓
Blue Pea Terrine	115	✓	✓	✓		
Bombay Sprouted Pea	118	✓	✓		✓	
Buckwheat Greens	58	✓	✓	✓	✓	✓
Buckwheat Groats Salad	59	✓	✓		✓	✓
Buckwheat Kasha Bread	64			✓		
Buckwheat Porridge	57	✓	✓	✓	✓	
Buckwheat Soba	62	✓	✓	✓	✓	
Buckwheat Cabbage Rolls	60	✓	✓	✓		
Buckwheat-Barley Pancakes	58	✓		✓		
Buckwheat-Corn Fritters	61	✓	✓	✓		
Chapati	26			✓	✓	
Cinnamon Rice Pudding	32	✓	✓	✓	✓	
Coconut Biscuits	52		✓	✓	✓	
Coeliac Fruit Cake	71	✓	✓	✓	✓	
Corn Sprout Muesli	89	✓	✓	✓	✓	✓
Cornbread	98	✓	✓	✓	✓	
Cornmeal Patties	94	✓	✓	✓		
Cornmeal Pie Shells	90	✓	✓	✓	✓	
Croissants	21					
Cucumber Raita	118	✓	✓		✓	✓
Danish Rice Pudding	31	✓	✓	✓	✓	
Date Oaties	108	✓	✓		✓	

Recipe	Page	Wheat Free	Gluten Free	Dairy Free	Yeast Free	Raw
Essene Bread	22			✓	✓	
Eyeball Ryeballs	40	✓		✓	✓	✓
Finest Cornmeal Porridge	89	✓	✓	✓	✓	
Fresh Herb Millet Salad	68	✓	✓	✓	✓	
Fresh Herbed Rice	30	✓	✓	✓	✓	
Fruity Freeze	104	✓	✓	✓	✓	✓
Georgious Barley Soup	79	✓		✓	✓	
Ginger Apple Muffins	74	✓	✓	✓	✓	
Gingerbread People	62	✓	✓	✓	✓	
Green Tomato Corncrust Pie	91	✓	✓	✓	✓	
Heavy Fruit Rye Bread	46	✓		✓		
Hot Sprout Breakfast	49	✓		✓	✓	
Indian Pea Stew	119	✓	✓	✓	✓	
Instant Pea Soup	116	✓	✓	✓	✓	
Ironsides Oatmeal Breakfast	101	✓		✓	✓	
Kasha	61	✓	✓	✓	✓	
Lebanese Pitta Bread	22			✓		
Lemon-Barley Water	77	✓		✓	✓	
Lemon-Oatmeal Soup	102	✓		✓		
Mediterranean Barley	82	✓			✓	
Mike McCammons Millet	68	✓	✓	✓		
Millet Banana Cake	72	✓	✓	✓	✓	
Millet Bread	73			✓		
Millet Muffins	72	✓	✓	✓	✓	
Millet Porridge	67	✓	✓	✓	✓	
Millet Stuffing for Peppers and Tomatoes	69	✓	✓	✓	✓	
No Knead Triticale Bread	54	✓		✓		
Oat Crunch	109	✓			✓	
Oat-Soy Burglars	103	✓		✓	✓	
Oat Sunrise	101	✓		✓	✓	✓
Oat Wafers	108	✓		✓	✓	
Oat-Rye Bread	110			✓		
Oatmeal Pie Dough	105	✓		✓		
Paprika-Sunflower Pâté	102	✓		✓	✓	✓
Pawpaw Raw Barley	82	✓		✓	✓	✓
Pea Stuffed Mushrooms	113	✓	✓	✓	✓	✓
Peaflour Pakoras	116	✓	✓	✓	✓	
Peanut Butter Pudding	95	✓	✓	✓	✓	
Peanut Coconut Biscuits	109	✓		✓	✓	
Pease Pudding	114	✓	✓	✓	✓	
Peasprout Sunbread	120			✓	✓	
Polenta	92	✓	✓	✓	✓	
Raw Banana Bread	53	✓		✓	✓	✓
Raw Fruit Cake	20			✓	✓	✓
Raw Fruit Chutney	23	✓	✓	✓	✓	✓

Recipe	Page	Wheat Free	Gluten Free	Dairy Free	Yeast Free	Raw
Raw Grain Muesli	15				✓	✓
Real Noodles	19			✓		
Rejuvelac	15			✓		✓
Rice Flour Banana Muffins	34	✓	✓	✓	✓	
Rice Sprout Breakfast	29	✓	✓	✓	✓	✓
Rice Tempura	29			✓	✓	
Rye & Barley Bread	43	✓		✓		
Rye and Peanut Porridge	39	✓		✓	✓	
Rye Rusks	42	✓		✓		
Rye Shortbread	43	✓			✓	
Rye-Tofu Pâté	40	✓		✓	✓	✓
Ryesprout Tomato Salad	39	✓		✓	✓	✓
Savoury Crackers	70	✓	✓	✓	✓	
Savoury Rice Biscuits	32	✓	✓	✓	✓	
Savoury Sesame Rice Crackers	34	✓	✓	✓	✓	
Simple Raw Tomato Sauce	79	✓	✓	✓	✓	✓
Sioux Pudding	97	✓	✓	✓	✓	
Spicy Maize Applecake	96	✓	✓	✓	✓	
Spinach Enchiladas	93	✓	✓	✓	✓	
Sprouted Pealaf	117	✓	✓	✓		
Sprouted Wheat and Red Pepper Salad	17			✓		✓
Sprouts Supreme	20			✓	✓	✓
Stir Fry Rye	41	✓		✓		
Superbale Triticale	49	✓			✓	✓
Syrian Herby Crispbread	25			✓		
Tabouli	18			✓	✓	
Tahini Pea Dip	113	✓	✓	✓	✓	✓
Tomatoes Stuffed with Wheat Sprouts	16				✓	✓
Tortillas	92	✓	✓	✓	✓	
Triticale Bumblebees	50	✓		✓		✓
Triticale Date Slice	53	✓			✓	
Triticale Fresh Fruit Pie	51	✓		✓	✓	
Triticale Lentil Pilaf	50	✓		✓	✓	
Triticale Shortbread	52	✓			✓	
Unleavened Rice Flour Carrot Cake	33	✓	✓	✓	✓	
Vege Tofu Curry on Millet	70	✓	✓	✓	✓	
Wheat Sprout Patties	18			✓	✓	
Whiteheart Sourdough Rye Bread	44	✓		✓		
Winter Wheat Porridge	16			✓	✓	

LIST OF SUPPLIERS

Organically grown grains and flours are becoming more readily available in New Zealand. We have listed the main sources; if your local shops cannot supply your needs we suggest contacting the nearest grower or wholesaler.

South Island

A.C. Maisey & Sons,
14 George Street,
Richmond, Nelson.
(Growers & millers)

Geoff Wilson,
Terrace Farm,
RD 12, Rakaia.
(Grower - Also mills Extra-Fine Flours)

Gerald Gates,
Trincomalee,
RD Amberley, Canterbury.
(Grower)

Ian Henderson,
Milmore Downs,
Amberley, Canterbury.
(Grower - Also mills Extra-Fine Flours)

Intrepid Seeds,
Rockford Gorge Road,
RD Oxford, Canterbury.
(Wholesalers)

John Scott,
Lancevale,Mason's Flat,
RD Hawarden, Canterbury.
(Grower - Also mills
stoneground flours)

New Zealand Biograins,
P.O. Box 526,Ashburton.
(Growers and millers)

Peter Buttle,
Dunfield,Hororata,
RD Darfield.
(Grower)

Riverside Grains,
Box 13,Hinds,
Mid Canterbury.
(Wholesalers)

Tim Chamberlain,
Lakeside,
RD Leeston, Canterbury.
(Grower)

North Island

Adrian White,
Millstream,
Pukehou,
Hawkes Bay.
(Grower)

Harmony Natural Foods
& Chico Mills,
Box 2405,Tauranga.
(Wholesalers & millers)

Jamie Tait-Jamieson,
RD 10,
Palmerston North.
(Grower)

Kai Ora Natural Foods,
Box 3007,
Auckland.
(Wholesalers & millers)

Mandala Foods,
1042 Cameron Road,
Tauranga,
(Co-op retailer)

Organic Food Co-op,
36 Arthur Street,
Wellington.
(Co-op retailer)

Peter Short,
Taumata,
RD 9, Fielding.
(Grower)

Other Useful Addresses

Biodynamic Association,
Box 306,
Napier.

New Zealand Biological Producers Council,
Box 25-350,
St Heliers Bay,
Auckland.

Permaculture New Zealand,
Box 37-030,
Parnell,
Auckland.

Soil Association,
Box 2824,
Auckland.

Bibliography and further reading

Grains, Beans, Nuts, by David Scott, Hutchinson, London.

Sprouts to Grow and Eat, by E. Munroe, Compendium Pty Ltd., Australia, 1984.

The Story of Ergot, by S. Karger, New York, 1970.

The Tassajara Bread Book, by E. E. Brown, Shambala Publications, 1973.

Technology of Cereals, by N. L. Kent, Pergamon, London, 1966.

The Allergy Self-Help Book, by M. Hart Jones, Rodale Press, U.S.A., 1984.

The Sprouting Book, by Ann Wigmore, Avery Publishing, New Jersey, U.S.A., 1986.

The Natural Food Catalogue, by Vicki Petersen, MacDonald & Co., London, 1984.